C-1931

THIS IS YOUR **PASSBOOK**® FOR ...

LIBRARY CLERK

NATIONAL LEARNING CORPORATION®
passbooks.com

Copyright © 2018 by

NLC®

National Learning Corporation

212 Michael Drive, Syosset, NY 11791
(516) 921-8888 • www.passbooks.com
E-mail: info@passbooks.com

PUBLISHED IN THE UNITED STATES OF AMERICA

PASSBOOK® SERIES

THE *PASSBOOK® SERIES* has been created to prepare applicants and candidates for the ultimate academic battlefield – the examination room.

At some time in our lives, each and every one of us may be required to take an examination – for validation, matriculation, admission, qualification, registration, certification, or licensure.

Based on the assumption that every applicant or candidate has met the basic formal educational standards, has taken the required number of courses, and read the necessary texts, the *PASSBOOK® SERIES* furnishes the one special preparation which may assure passing with confidence, instead of failing with insecurity. Examination questions – together with answers – are furnished as the basic vehicle for study so that the mysteries of the examination and its compounding difficulties may be eliminated or diminished by a sure method.

This book is meant to help you pass your examination provided that you qualify and are serious in your objective.

The entire field is reviewed through the huge store of content information which is succinctly presented through a provocative and challenging approach – the question-and-answer method.

A climate of success is established by furnishing the correct answers at the end of each test.

You soon learn to recognize types of questions, forms of questions, and patterns of questioning. You may even begin to anticipate expected outcomes.

You perceive that many questions are repeated or adapted so that you can gain acute insights, which may enable you to score many sure points.

You learn how to confront new questions, or types of questions, and to attack them confidently and work out the correct answers.

You note objectives and emphases, and recognize pitfalls and dangers, so that you may make positive educational adjustments.

Moreover, you are kept fully informed in relation to new concepts, methods, practices, and directions in the field.

You discover that you arre actually taking the examination all the time: you are preparing for the examination by "taking" an examination, not by reading extraneous and/or supererogatory textbooks.

In short, this PASSBOOK®, used directedly, should be an important factor in helping you to pass your test.

LIBRARY CLERK

DUTIES:

The work involves the performance of routine library clerical duties necessary for the proper organization and distribution of library provided. Work is performed under direct supervision of higher level clerks or librarians. Candidate may supervise pages and volunteers. Performs clerical duties in a public library and assists library patrons in using the materials and equipment in the library; arranges or files materials according to library filing rules; performs routine searches of and updates to computer records; issues borrowers cards according to library procedures; performs routine circulation, reserve and overdue functions; makes and checks routine arithmetic computations; answers the telephone and takes messages; calls patrons to deliver messages or information on library materials; types cards, lists, labels, or short entries on forms. Performs related work as required.

TYPICAL WORK ACTIVITIES:

Typical work activities include, but are not limited to the following: Arrange and/or file materials according to library filing rules; Perform routine searches of, and updates to, computer records; Issue borrowers cards according to library procedures; Perform routine circulation, reserve and overdue functions; Make and check routine arithmetic computations; Operate office machinery such as photocopiers, fax machines or computers; Answer the telephone and takes messages; Call patrons two deliver messages or information on library materials; Type cards, lists, labels, or short entries on forms. The following full performance knowledge, skills, abilities and personal characteristics are expected of candidate: Working knowledge of office terminology, procedures and equipment as it applies to library clerical work; a working knowledge of library filing and shelving rules; the ability to understand and follow oral and written instructions; the ability to operate an alphanumeric keyboard such as a typewriter, terminal, or personal computer accurately—skilled typing is not necessary; tact and courtesy in dealing with staff and public.

EXAMPLES OF WORK:

- Serves at the circulation desk issuing, renewing and receiving library materials;
- Shelves magazines, books and inspects shelves to maintain proper catalog order;
- Processes new books by preparing call numbers, catalog cards, shelf list, pockets, book cards and jackets;
- Files catalog cards, overdue notices, magazines, shelf list cards, supply catalogs and other materials;
- Issues borrowers identification card according to established procedures;
- Processes overdue books by calling patrons, sending reminders, bills, etc.;
- Takes reserve orders from patrons via telephone and in person;
- Serves as primary media services contact for library patrons and processes requests for multi-media services;
- Processes purchasing request for the multi-media center;
- Operates media equipment such as projectors, audio recorders, video records, etc.;
- Develops and maintains a database of booklets, catalogs and other resource material;
- Packs and unpacks media materials;
- Enters and retrieves information using a computer terminal and standard catalog card file;
- Receives, checks and catalogs library materials such as periodicals, books and audio-visual material;
- Issues audio-visual equipment for use in the library;

- May type cards, lists, labels, etc., not requiring skilled typing;
- Assists patrons in utilizing Library search methods and helps patrons locate materials;
- May assist Librarian in preparing displays to promote reading activities;
- Prepares a variety of related reports and records.

SCOPE OF THE EXAMINATION
The written test will be designed to test for knowledge, skills and/or abilities in such areas as:
1. Clerical operations with letters and numbers;
2. Alphabetizing;
3. Record keeping; and
4. Spelling, punctuation and capitalization.

HOW TO TAKE A TEST

I. YOU MUST PASS AN EXAMINATION

A. WHAT EVERY CANDIDATE SHOULD KNOW

Examination applicants often ask us for help in preparing for the written test. What can I study in advance? What kinds of questions will be asked? How will the test be given? How will the papers be graded?

As an applicant for a civil service examination, you may be wondering about some of these things. Our purpose here is to suggest effective methods of advance study and to describe civil service examinations.

Your chances for success on this examination can be increased if you know how to prepare. Those "pre-examination jitters" can be reduced if you know what to expect. You can even experience an adventure in good citizenship if you know why civil service exams are given.

B. WHY ARE CIVIL SERVICE EXAMINATIONS GIVEN?

Civil service examinations are important to you in two ways. As a citizen, you want public jobs filled by employees who know how to do their work. As a job seeker, you want a fair chance to compete for that job on an equal footing with other candidates. The best-known means of accomplishing this two-fold goal is the competitive examination.

Exams are widely publicized throughout the nation. They may be administered for jobs in federal, state, city, municipal, town or village governments or agencies.

Any citizen may apply, with some limitations, such as the age or residence of applicants. Your experience and education may be reviewed to see whether you meet the requirements for the particular examination. When these requirements exist, they are reasonable and applied consistently to all applicants. Thus, a competitive examination may cause you some uneasiness now, but it is your privilege and safeguard.

C. HOW ARE CIVIL SERVICE EXAMS DEVELOPED?

Examinations are carefully written by trained technicians who are specialists in the field known as "psychological measurement," in consultation with recognized authorities in the field of work that the test will cover. These experts recommend the subject matter areas or skills to be tested; only those knowledges or skills important to your success on the job are included. The most reliable books and source materials available are used as references. Together, the experts and technicians judge the difficulty level of the questions.

Test technicians know how to phrase questions so that the problem is clearly stated. Their ethics do not permit "trick" or "catch" questions. Questions may have been tried out on sample groups, or subjected to statistical analysis, to determine their usefulness.

Written tests are often used in combination with performance tests, ratings of training and experience, and oral interviews. All of these measures combine to form the best-known means of finding the right person for the right job.

II. HOW TO PASS THE WRITTEN TEST

A. NATURE OF THE EXAMINATION

To prepare intelligently for civil service examinations, you should know how they differ from school examinations you have taken. In school you were assigned certain definite pages to read or subjects to cover. The examination questions were quite detailed and usually emphasized memory. Civil service exams, on the other hand, try to discover your present ability to perform the duties of a position, plus your potentiality to learn these duties. In other words, a civil service exam attempts to predict how successful you will be. Questions cover such a broad area that they cannot be as minute and detailed as school exam questions.

In the public service similar kinds of work, or positions, are grouped together in one "class." This process is known as *position-classification*. All the positions in a class are paid according to the salary range for that class. One class title covers all of these positions, and they are all tested by the same examination.

B. FOUR BASIC STEPS

1) Study the announcement

How, then, can you know what subjects to study? Our best answer is: "Learn as much as possible about the class of positions for which you've applied." The exam will test the knowledge, skills and abilities needed to do the work.

Your most valuable source of information about the position you want is the official exam announcement. This announcement lists the training and experience qualifications. Check these standards and apply only if you come reasonably close to meeting them.

The brief description of the position in the examination announcement offers some clues to the subjects which will be tested. Think about the job itself. Review the duties in your mind. Can you perform them, or are there some in which you are rusty? Fill in the blank spots in your preparation.

Many jurisdictions preview the written test in the exam announcement by including a section called "Knowledge and Abilities Required," "Scope of the Examination," or some similar heading. Here you will find out specifically what fields will be tested.

2) Review your own background

Once you learn in general what the position is all about, and what you need to know to do the work, ask yourself which subjects you already know fairly well and which need improvement. You may wonder whether to concentrate on improving your strong areas or on building some background in your fields of weakness. When the announcement has specified "some knowledge" or "considerable knowledge," or has used adjectives like "beginning principles of…" or "advanced … methods," you can get a clue as to the number and difficulty of questions to be asked in any given field. More questions, and hence broader coverage, would be included for those subjects which are more important in the work. Now weigh your strengths and weaknesses against the job requirements and prepare accordingly.

3) Determine the level of the position

Another way to tell how intensively you should prepare is to understand the level of the job for which you are applying. Is it the entering level? In other words, is this the position in which beginners in a field of work are hired? Or is it an intermediate or advanced level? Sometimes this is indicated by such words as "Junior" or "Senior" in the class title. Other jurisdictions use Roman numerals to designate the level – Clerk I, Clerk II, for example. The word "Supervisor" sometimes appears in the title. If the level is not indicated by the title, check the description of duties. Will you be working under very close supervision, or will you have responsibility for independent decisions in this work?

4) Choose appropriate study materials

Now that you know the subjects to be examined and the relative amount of each subject to be covered, you can choose suitable study materials. For beginning level jobs, or even advanced ones, if you have a pronounced weakness in some aspect of your training, read a modern, standard textbook in that field. Be sure it is up to date and has general coverage. Such books are normally available at your library, and the librarian will be glad to help you locate one. For entry-level positions, questions of appropriate difficulty are chosen – neither highly advanced questions, nor those too simple. Such questions require careful thought but not advanced training.

If the position for which you are applying is technical or advanced, you will read more advanced, specialized material. If you are already familiar with the basic principles of your field, elementary textbooks would waste your time. Concentrate on advanced textbooks and technical periodicals. Think through the concepts and review difficult problems in your field.

These are all general sources. You can get more ideas on your own initiative, following these leads. For example, training manuals and publications of the government agency which employs workers in your field can be useful, particularly for technical and professional positions. A letter or visit to the government department involved may result in more specific study suggestions, and certainly will provide you with a more definite idea of the exact nature of the position you are seeking.

III. KINDS OF TESTS

Tests are used for purposes other than measuring knowledge and ability to perform specified duties. For some positions, it is equally important to test ability to make adjustments to new situations or to profit from training. In others, basic mental abilities not dependent on information are essential. Questions which test these things may not appear as pertinent to the duties of the position as those which test for knowledge and information. Yet they are often highly important parts of a fair examination. For very general questions, it is almost impossible to help you direct your study efforts. What we can do is to point out some of the more common of these general abilities needed in public service positions and describe some typical questions.

1) General information

Broad, general information has been found useful for predicting job success in some kinds of work. This is tested in a variety of ways, from vocabulary lists to questions about current events. Basic background in some field of work, such as sociology or economics, may be sampled in a group of questions. Often these are principles which have become familiar to most persons through exposure rather than through formal training. It is difficult to advise you how to study for these questions; being alert to the world around you is our best suggestion.

2) Verbal ability

An example of an ability needed in many positions is verbal or language ability. Verbal ability is, in brief, the ability to use and understand words. Vocabulary and grammar tests are typical measures of this ability. Reading comprehension or paragraph interpretation questions are common in many kinds of civil service tests. You are given a paragraph of written material and asked to find its central meaning.

3) Numerical ability

Number skills can be tested by the familiar arithmetic problem, by checking paired lists of numbers to see which are alike and which are different, or by interpreting charts and graphs. In the latter test, a graph may be printed in the test booklet which you are asked to use as the basis for answering questions.

4) Observation

A popular test for law-enforcement positions is the observation test. A picture is shown to you for several minutes, then taken away. Questions about the picture test your ability to observe both details and larger elements.

5) Following directions

In many positions in the public service, the employee must be able to carry out written instructions dependably and accurately. You may be given a chart with several columns, each column listing a variety of information. The questions require you to carry out directions involving the information given in the chart.

6) Skills and aptitudes

Performance tests effectively measure some manual skills and aptitudes. When the skill is one in which you are trained, such as typing or shorthand, you can practice. These tests are often very much like those given in business school or high school courses. For many of the other skills and aptitudes, however, no short-time preparation can be made. Skills and abilities natural to you or that you have developed throughout your lifetime are being tested.

Many of the general questions just described provide all the data needed to answer the questions and ask you to use your reasoning ability to find the answers. Your best preparation for these tests, as well as for tests of facts and ideas, is to be at your physical and mental best. You, no doubt, have your own methods of getting into an exam-taking mood and keeping "in shape." The next section lists some ideas on this subject.

IV. KINDS OF QUESTIONS

Only rarely is the "essay" question, which you answer in narrative form, used in civil service tests. Civil service tests are usually of the short-answer type. Full instructions for answering these questions will be given to you at the examination. But in case this is your first experience with short-answer questions and separate answer sheets, here is what you need to know:

1) Multiple-choice Questions

Most popular of the short-answer questions is the "multiple choice" or "best answer" question. It can be used, for example, to test for factual knowledge, ability to solve problems or judgment in meeting situations found at work.

A multiple-choice question is normally one of three types—

- It can begin with an incomplete statement followed by several possible endings. You are to find the one ending which *best* completes the statement, although some of the others may not be entirely wrong.
- It can also be a complete statement in the form of a question which is answered by choosing one of the statements listed.
- It can be in the form of a problem – again you select the best answer.

Here is an example of a multiple-choice question with a discussion which should give you some clues as to the method for choosing the right answer:

When an employee has a complaint about his assignment, the action which will *best* help him overcome his difficulty is to
A. discuss his difficulty with his coworkers
B. take the problem to the head of the organization
C. take the problem to the person who gave him the assignment
D. say nothing to anyone about his complaint

In answering this question, you should study each of the choices to find which is best. Consider choice "A" – Certainly an employee may discuss his complaint with fellow employees, but no change or improvement can result, and the complaint remains unresolved. Choice "B" is a poor choice since the head of the organization probably does not know what assignment you have been given, and taking your problem to him is known as "going over the head" of the supervisor. The supervisor, or person who made the assignment, is the person who can clarify it or correct any injustice. Choice "C" is, therefore, correct. To say nothing, as in choice "D," is unwise. Supervisors have and interest in knowing the problems employees are facing, and the employee is seeking a solution to his problem.

2) True/False Questions

The "true/false" or "right/wrong" form of question is sometimes used. Here a complete statement is given. Your job is to decide whether the statement is right or wrong.

SAMPLE: A roaming cell-phone call to a nearby city costs less than a non-roaming call to a distant city.

This statement is wrong, or false, since roaming calls are more expensive.
This is not a complete list of all possible question forms, although most of the others are variations of these common types. You will always get complete directions for

answering questions. Be sure you understand *how* to mark your answers – ask questions until you do.

V. RECORDING YOUR ANSWERS

Computer terminals are used more and more today for many different kinds of exams.

For an examination with very few applicants, you may be told to record your answers in the test booklet itself. Separate answer sheets are much more common. If this separate answer sheet is to be scored by machine – and this is often the case – it is highly important that you mark your answers correctly in order to get credit.

An electronic scoring machine is often used in civil service offices because of the speed with which papers can be scored. Machine-scored answer sheets must be marked with a pencil, which will be given to you. This pencil has a high graphite content which responds to the electronic scoring machine. As a matter of fact, stray dots may register as answers, so do not let your pencil rest on the answer sheet while you are pondering the correct answer. Also, if your pencil lead breaks or is otherwise defective, ask for another.

Since the answer sheet will be dropped in a slot in the scoring machine, be careful not to bend the corners or get the paper crumpled.

The answer sheet normally has five vertical columns of numbers, with 30 numbers to a column. These numbers correspond to the question numbers in your test booklet. After each number, going across the page are four or five pairs of dotted lines. These short dotted lines have small letters or numbers above them. The first two pairs may also have a "T" or "F" above the letters. This indicates that the first two pairs only are to be used if the questions are of the true-false type. If the questions are multiple choice, disregard the "T" and "F" and pay attention only to the small letters or numbers.

Answer your questions in the manner of the sample that follows:

32. The largest city in the United States is
      A. Washington, D.C.
      B. New York City
      C. Chicago
      D. Detroit
      E. San Francisco

1) Choose the answer you think is best. (New York City is the largest, so "B" is correct.)
2) Find the row of dotted lines numbered the same as the question you are answering. (Find row number 32)
3) Find the pair of dotted lines corresponding to the answer. (Find the pair of lines under the mark "B.")
4) Make a solid black mark between the dotted lines.

VI. BEFORE THE TEST

Common sense will help you find procedures to follow to get ready for an examination. Too many of us, however, overlook these sensible measures. Indeed, nervousness and fatigue have been found to be the most serious reasons why applicants fail to do their best on civil service tests. Here is a list of reminders:

- Begin your preparation early – Don't wait until the last minute to go scurrying around for books and materials or to find out what the position is all about.
- Prepare continuously – An hour a night for a week is better than an all-night cram session. This has been definitely established. What is more, a night a week for a month will return better dividends than crowding your study into a shorter period of time.
- Locate the place of the exam – You have been sent a notice telling you when and where to report for the examination. If the location is in a different town or otherwise unfamiliar to you, it would be well to inquire the best route and learn something about the building.
- Relax the night before the test – Allow your mind to rest. Do not study at all that night. Plan some mild recreation or diversion; then go to bed early and get a good night's sleep.
- Get up early enough to make a leisurely trip to the place for the test – This way unforeseen events, traffic snarls, unfamiliar buildings, etc. will not upset you.
- Dress comfortably – A written test is not a fashion show. You will be known by number and not by name, so wear something comfortable.
- Leave excess paraphernalia at home – Shopping bags and odd bundles will get in your way. You need bring only the items mentioned in the official notice you received; usually everything you need is provided. Do not bring reference books to the exam. They will only confuse those last minutes and be taken away from you when in the test room.
- Arrive somewhat ahead of time – If because of transportation schedules you must get there very early, bring a newspaper or magazine to take your mind off yourself while waiting.
- Locate the examination room – When you have found the proper room, you will be directed to the seat or part of the room where you will sit. Sometimes you are given a sheet of instructions to read while you are waiting. Do not fill out any forms until you are told to do so; just read them and be prepared.
- Relax and prepare to listen to the instructions
- If you have any physical problem that may keep you from doing your best, be sure to tell the test administrator. If you are sick or in poor health, you really cannot do your best on the exam. You can come back and take the test some other time.

VII. AT THE TEST

The day of the test is here and you have the test booklet in your hand. The temptation to get going is very strong. Caution! There is more to success than knowing the right answers. You must know how to identify your papers and understand variations in the type of short-answer question used in this particular examination. Follow these suggestions for maximum results from your efforts:

1) Cooperate with the monitor

The test administrator has a duty to create a situation in which you can be as much at ease as possible. He will give instructions, tell you when to begin, check to see that you are marking your answer sheet correctly, and so on. He is not there to guard you, although he will see that your competitors do not take unfair advantage. He wants to help you do your best.

2) Listen to all instructions

Don't jump the gun! Wait until you understand all directions. In most civil service tests you get more time than you need to answer the questions. So don't be in a hurry. Read each word of instructions until you clearly understand the meaning. Study the examples, listen to all announcements and follow directions. Ask questions if you do not understand what to do.

3) Identify your papers

Civil service exams are usually identified by number only. You will be assigned a number; you must not put your name on your test papers. Be sure to copy your number correctly. Since more than one exam may be given, copy your exact examination title.

4) Plan your time

Unless you are told that a test is a "speed" or "rate of work" test, speed itself is usually not important. Time enough to answer all the questions will be provided, but this does not mean that you have all day. An overall time limit has been set. Divide the total time (in minutes) by the number of questions to determine the approximate time you have for each question.

5) Do not linger over difficult questions

If you come across a difficult question, mark it with a paper clip (useful to have along) and come back to it when you have been through the booklet. One caution if you do this – be sure to skip a number on your answer sheet as well. Check often to be sure that you have not lost your place and that you are marking in the row numbered the same as the question you are answering.

6) Read the questions

Be sure you know what the question asks! Many capable people are unsuccessful because they failed to *read* the questions correctly.

7) Answer all questions

Unless you have been instructed that a penalty will be deducted for incorrect answers, it is better to guess than to omit a question.

8) Speed tests

It is often better NOT to guess on speed tests. It has been found that on timed tests people are tempted to spend the last few seconds before time is called in marking answers at random – without even reading them – in the hope of picking up a few extra points. To discourage this practice, the instructions may warn you that your score will be "corrected" for guessing. That is, a penalty will be applied. The incorrect answers will be deducted from the correct ones, or some other penalty formula will be used.

9) Review your answers

If you finish before time is called, go back to the questions you guessed or omitted to give them further thought. Review other answers if you have time.

10) Return your test materials

If you are ready to leave before others have finished or time is called, take ALL your materials to the monitor and leave quietly. Never take any test material with you. The monitor can discover whose papers are not complete, and taking a test booklet may be grounds for disqualification.

VIII. EXAMINATION TECHNIQUES

1) Read the general instructions carefully. These are usually printed on the first page of the exam booklet. As a rule, these instructions refer to the timing of the examination; the fact that you should not start work until the signal and must stop work at a signal, etc. If there are any *special* instructions, such as a choice of questions to be answered, make sure that you note this instruction carefully.

2) When you are ready to start work on the examination, that is as soon as the signal has been given, read the instructions to each question booklet, underline any key words or phrases, such as *least, best, outline, describe* and the like. In this way you will tend to answer as requested rather than discover on reviewing your paper that you *listed without describing*, that you selected the *worst* choice rather than the *best* choice, etc.

3) If the examination is of the objective or multiple-choice type – that is, each question will also give a series of possible answers: A, B, C or D, and you are called upon to select the best answer and write the letter next to that answer on your answer paper – it is advisable to start answering each question in turn. There may be anywhere from 50 to 100 such questions in the three or four hours allotted and you can see how much time would be taken if you read through all the questions before beginning to answer any. Furthermore, if you come across a question or group of questions which you know would be difficult to answer, it would undoubtedly affect your handling of all the other questions.

4) If the examination is of the essay type and contains but a few questions, it is a moot point as to whether you should read all the questions before starting to answer any one. Of course, if you are given a choice – say five out of seven and the like – then it is essential to read all the questions so you can eliminate the two that are most difficult. If, however, you are asked to answer all the questions, there may be danger in trying to answer the easiest one first because you may find that you will spend too much time on it. The best technique is to answer the first question, then proceed to the second, etc.

5) Time your answers. Before the exam begins, write down the time it started, then add the time allowed for the examination and write down the time it must be completed, then divide the time available somewhat as follows:

- If 3-1/2 hours are allowed, that would be 210 minutes. If you have 80 objective-type questions, that would be an average of 2-1/2 minutes per question. Allow yourself no more than 2 minutes per question, or a total of 160 minutes, which will permit about 50 minutes to review.
- If for the time allotment of 210 minutes there are 7 essay questions to answer, that would average about 30 minutes a question. Give yourself only 25 minutes per question so that you have about 35 minutes to review.

6) The most important instruction is to *read each question* and make sure you know what is wanted. The second most important instruction is to *time yourself properly* so that you answer every question. The third most important instruction is to *answer every question*. Guess if you have to but include something for each question. Remember that you will receive no credit for a blank and will probably receive some credit if you write something in answer to an essay question. If you guess a letter – say "B" for a multiple-choice question – you may have guessed right. If you leave a blank as an answer to a multiple-choice question, the examiners may respect your feelings but it will not add a point to your score. Some exams may penalize you for wrong answers, so in such cases *only*, you may not want to guess unless you have some basis for your answer.

7) Suggestions
   a. Objective-type questions
      1. Examine the question booklet for proper sequence of pages and questions
      2. Read all instructions carefully
      3. Skip any question which seems too difficult; return to it after all other questions have been answered
      4. Apportion your time properly; do not spend too much time on any single question or group of questions
      5. Note and underline key words – *all, most, fewest, least, best, worst, same, opposite,* etc.
      6. Pay particular attention to negatives
      7. Note unusual option, e.g., unduly long, short, complex, different or similar in content to the body of the question
      8. Observe the use of "hedging" words – *probably, may, most likely,* etc.
      9. Make sure that your answer is put next to the same number as the question
      10. Do not second-guess unless you have good reason to believe the second answer is definitely more correct
      11. Cross out original answer if you decide another answer is more accurate; do not erase until you are ready to hand your paper in
      12. Answer all questions; guess unless instructed otherwise
      13. Leave time for review

   b. Essay questions
      1. Read each question carefully
      2. Determine exactly what is wanted. Underline key words or phrases.
      3. Decide on outline or paragraph answer

4. Include many different points and elements unless asked to develop any one or two points or elements
5. Show impartiality by giving pros and cons unless directed to select one side only
6. Make and write down any assumptions you find necessary to answer the questions
7. Watch your English, grammar, punctuation and choice of words
8. Time your answers; don't crowd material

8) Answering the essay question

Most essay questions can be answered by framing the specific response around several key words or ideas. Here are a few such key words or ideas:

M's: manpower, materials, methods, money, management
P's: purpose, program, policy, plan, procedure, practice, problems, pitfalls, personnel, public relations
  a. Six basic steps in handling problems:
     1. Preliminary plan and background development
     2. Collect information, data and facts
     3. Analyze and interpret information, data and facts
     4. Analyze and develop solutions as well as make recommendations
     5. Prepare report and sell recommendations
     6. Install recommendations and follow up effectiveness

  b. Pitfalls to avoid
     1. *Taking things for granted* – A statement of the situation does not necessarily imply that each of the elements is necessarily true; for example, a complaint may be invalid and biased so that all that can be taken for granted is that a complaint has been registered
     2. *Considering only one side of a situation* – Wherever possible, indicate several alternatives and then point out the reasons you selected the best one
     3. *Failing to indicate follow up* – Whenever your answer indicates action on your part, make certain that you will take proper follow-up action to see how successful your recommendations, procedures or actions turn out to be
     4. *Taking too long in answering any single question* – Remember to time your answers properly

IX. AFTER THE TEST

Scoring procedures differ in detail among civil service jurisdictions although the general principles are the same. Whether the papers are hand-scored or graded by machine we have described, they are nearly always graded by number. That is, the person who marks the paper knows only the number – never the name – of the applicant. Not until all the papers have been graded will they be matched with names. If other tests, such as training and experience or oral interview ratings have been given, scores will be combined. Different parts of the examination usually have different weights. For example, the written test might count 60 percent of the final grade, and a rating of training and experience 40 percent. In many jurisdictions, veterans will have a certain number of points added to their grades.

After the final grade has been determined, the names are placed in grade order and an eligible list is established. There are various methods for resolving ties between those who get the same final grade – probably the most common is to place first the name of the person whose application was received first. Job offers are made from the eligible list in the order the names appear on it. You will be notified of your grade and your rank as soon as all these computations have been made. This will be done as rapidly as possible.

People who are found to meet the requirements in the announcement are called "eligibles." Their names are put on a list of eligible candidates. An eligible's chances of getting a job depend on how high he stands on this list and how fast agencies are filling jobs from the list.

When a job is to be filled from a list of eligibles, the agency asks for the names of people on the list of eligibles for that job. When the civil service commission receives this request, it sends to the agency the names of the three people highest on this list. Or, if the job to be filled has specialized requirements, the office sends the agency the names of the top three persons who meet these requirements from the general list.

The appointing officer makes a choice from among the three people whose names were sent to him. If the selected person accepts the appointment, the names of the others are put back on the list to be considered for future openings.

That is the rule in hiring from all kinds of eligible lists, whether they are for typist, carpenter, chemist, or something else. For every vacancy, the appointing officer has his choice of any one of the top three eligibles on the list. This explains why the person whose name is on top of the list sometimes does not get an appointment when some of the persons lower on the list do. If the appointing officer chooses the second or third eligible, the No. 1 eligible does not get a job at once, but stays on the list until he is appointed or the list is terminated.

X. HOW TO PASS THE INTERVIEW TEST

The examination for which you applied requires an oral interview test. You have already taken the written test and you are now being called for the interview test – the final part of the formal examination.

You may think that it is not possible to prepare for an interview test and that there are no procedures to follow during an interview. Our purpose is to point out some things you can do in advance that will help you and some good rules to follow and pitfalls to avoid while you are being interviewed.

What is an interview supposed to test?

The written examination is designed to test the technical knowledge and competence of the candidate; the oral is designed to evaluate intangible qualities, not readily measured otherwise, and to establish a list showing the relative fitness of each candidate – as measured against his competitors – for the position sought. Scoring is not on the basis of "right" and "wrong," but on a sliding scale of values ranging from "not passable" to "outstanding." As a matter of fact, it is possible to achieve a relatively low score without a single "incorrect" answer because of evident weakness in the qualities being measured.

Occasionally, an examination may consist entirely of an oral test – either an individual or a group oral. In such cases, information is sought concerning the technical knowledges and abilities of the candidate, since there has been no written examination for this purpose. More commonly, however, an oral test is used to supplement a written examination.

Who conducts interviews?

The composition of oral boards varies among different jurisdictions. In nearly all, a representative of the personnel department serves as chairman. One of the members of the board may be a representative of the department in which the candidate would work. In some cases, "outside experts" are used, and, frequently, a businessman or some other representative of the general public is asked to serve. Labor and management or other special groups may be represented. The aim is to secure the services of experts in the appropriate field.

However the board is composed, it is a good idea (and not at all improper or unethical) to ascertain in advance of the interview who the members are and what groups they represent. When you are introduced to them, you will have some idea of their backgrounds and interests, and at least you will not stutter and stammer over their names.

What should be done before the interview?

While knowledge about the board members is useful and takes some of the surprise element out of the interview, there is other preparation which is more substantive. It *is* possible to prepare for an oral interview – in several ways:

1) Keep a copy of your application and review it carefully before the interview

This may be the only document before the oral board, and the starting point of the interview. Know what education and experience you have listed there, and the sequence and dates of all of it. Sometimes the board will ask you to review the highlights of your experience for them; you should not have to hem and haw doing it.

2) Study the class specification and the examination announcement

Usually, the oral board has one or both of these to guide them. The qualities, characteristics or knowledges required by the position sought are stated in these documents. They offer valuable clues as to the nature of the oral interview. For example, if the job involves supervisory responsibilities, the announcement will usually indicate that knowledge of modern supervisory methods and the qualifications of the candidate as a supervisor will be tested. If so, you can expect such questions, frequently in the form of a hypothetical situation which you are expected to solve. NEVER go into an oral without knowledge of the duties and responsibilities of the job you seek.

3) Think through each qualification required

Try to visualize the kind of questions you would ask if you were a board member. How well could you answer them? Try especially to appraise your own knowledge and background in each area, *measured against the job sought*, and identify any areas in which you are weak. Be critical and realistic – do not flatter yourself.

4) Do some general reading in areas in which you feel you may be weak

For example, if the job involves supervision and your past experience has NOT, some general reading in supervisory methods and practices, particularly in the field of human relations, might be useful. Do NOT study agency procedures or detailed manuals. The oral board will be testing your understanding and capacity, not your memory.

5) Get a good night's sleep and watch your general health and mental attitude

You will want a clear head at the interview. Take care of a cold or any other minor ailment, and of course, no hangovers.

What should be done on the day of the interview?

Now comes the day of the interview itself. Give yourself plenty of time to get there. Plan to arrive somewhat ahead of the scheduled time, particularly if your appointment is in the fore part of the day. If a previous candidate fails to appear, the board might be ready for you a bit early. By early afternoon an oral board is almost invariably behind schedule if there are many candidates, and you may have to wait. Take along a book or magazine to read, or your application to review, but leave any extraneous material in the waiting room when you go in for your interview. In any event, relax and compose yourself.

The matter of dress is important. The board is forming impressions about you – from your experience, your manners, your attitude, and your appearance. Give your personal appearance careful attention. Dress your best, but not your flashiest. Choose conservative, appropriate clothing, and be sure it is immaculate. This is a business interview, and your appearance should indicate that you regard it as such. Besides, being well groomed and properly dressed will help boost your confidence.

Sooner or later, someone will call your name and escort you into the interview room. *This is it.* From here on you are on your own. It is too late for any more preparation. But remember, you asked for this opportunity to prove your fitness, and you are here because your request was granted.

What happens when you go in?

The usual sequence of events will be as follows: The clerk (who is often the board stenographer) will introduce you to the chairman of the oral board, who will introduce you to the other members of the board. Acknowledge the introductions before you sit down. Do not be surprised if you find a microphone facing you or a stenotypist sitting by. Oral interviews are usually recorded in the event of an appeal or other review.

Usually the chairman of the board will open the interview by reviewing the highlights of your education and work experience from your application – primarily for the benefit of the other members of the board, as well as to get the material into the record. Do not interrupt or comment unless there is an error or significant misinterpretation; if that is the case, do not hesitate. But do not quibble about insignificant matters. Also, he will usually ask you some question about your education, experience or your present job – partly to get you to start talking and to establish the interviewing "rapport." He may start the actual questioning, or turn it over to one of the other members. Frequently, each member undertakes the questioning on a particular area, one in which he is perhaps most competent, so you can expect each member to participate in the examination. Because time is limited, you may also expect some rather abrupt switches in the direction the questioning takes, so do not be upset by it. Normally, a board member will not pursue a single line of questioning unless he discovers a particular strength or weakness.

After each member has participated, the chairman will usually ask whether any member has any further questions, then will ask you if you have anything you wish to add. Unless you are expecting this question, it may floor you. Worse, it may start you off on an extended, extemporaneous speech. The board is not usually seeking more information. The question is principally to offer you a last opportunity to present further qualifications or to indicate that you have nothing to add. So, if you feel that a significant qualification or characteristic has been overlooked, it is proper to point it out in a sentence or so. Do not compliment the board on the thoroughness of their examination – they have been sketchy, and you know it. If you wish, merely say, "No thank you, I have nothing further to add." This is a point where you can "talk yourself out" of a good impression or fail to present an important bit of information. Remember, *you close the interview yourself.*

The chairman will then say, "That is all, Mr. _____, thank you." Do not be startled; the interview is over, and quicker than you think. Thank him, gather your belongings and take your leave. Save your sigh of relief for the other side of the door.

How to put your best foot forward

Throughout this entire process, you may feel that the board individually and collectively is trying to pierce your defenses, seek out your hidden weaknesses and embarrass and confuse you. Actually, this is not true. They are obliged to make an appraisal of your qualifications for the job you are seeking, and they want to see you in your best light. Remember, they must interview all candidates and a non-cooperative candidate may become a failure in spite of their best efforts to bring out his qualifications. Here are 15 suggestions that will help you:

1) Be natural – Keep your attitude confident, not cocky

If you are not confident that you can do the job, do not expect the board to be. Do not apologize for your weaknesses, try to bring out your strong points. The board is interested in a positive, not negative, presentation. Cockiness will antagonize any board member and make him wonder if you are covering up a weakness by a false show of strength.

2) Get comfortable, but don't lounge or sprawl

Sit erectly but not stiffly. A careless posture may lead the board to conclude that you are careless in other things, or at least that you are not impressed by the importance of the occasion. Either conclusion is natural, even if incorrect. Do not fuss with your clothing, a pencil or an ashtray. Your hands may occasionally be useful to emphasize a point; do not let them become a point of distraction.

3) Do not wisecrack or make small talk

This is a serious situation, and your attitude should show that you consider it as such. Further, the time of the board is limited – they do not want to waste it, and neither should you.

4) Do not exaggerate your experience or abilities

In the first place, from information in the application or other interviews and sources, the board may know more about you than you think. Secondly, you probably will not get away with it. An experienced board is rather adept at spotting such a situation, so do not take the chance.

5) If you know a board member, do not make a point of it, yet do not hide it

Certainly you are not fooling him, and probably not the other members of the board. Do not try to take advantage of your acquaintanceship – it will probably do you little good.

6) Do not dominate the interview

Let the board do that. They will give you the clues – do not assume that you have to do all the talking. Realize that the board has a number of questions to ask you, and do not try to take up all the interview time by showing off your extensive knowledge of the answer to the first one.

7) Be attentive

You only have 20 minutes or so, and you should keep your attention at its sharpest throughout. When a member is addressing a problem or question to you, give him your undivided attention. Address your reply principally to him, but do not exclude the other board members.

8) Do not interrupt

A board member may be stating a problem for you to analyze. He will ask you a question when the time comes. Let him state the problem, and wait for the question.

9) Make sure you understand the question

Do not try to answer until you are sure what the question is. If it is not clear, restate it in your own words or ask the board member to clarify it for you. However, do not haggle about minor elements.

10) Reply promptly but not hastily

A common entry on oral board rating sheets is "candidate responded readily," or "candidate hesitated in replies." Respond as promptly and quickly as you can, but do not jump to a hasty, ill-considered answer.

11) Do not be peremptory in your answers

A brief answer is proper – but do not fire your answer back. That is a losing game from your point of view. The board member can probably ask questions much faster than you can answer them.

12) Do not try to create the answer you think the board member wants

He is interested in what kind of mind you have and how it works – not in playing games. Furthermore, he can usually spot this practice and will actually grade you down on it.

13) Do not switch sides in your reply merely to agree with a board member

Frequently, a member will take a contrary position merely to draw you out and to see if you are willing and able to defend your point of view. Do not start a debate, yet do not surrender a good position. If a position is worth taking, it is worth defending.

14) Do not be afraid to admit an error in judgment if you are shown to be wrong

The board knows that you are forced to reply without any opportunity for careful consideration. Your answer may be demonstrably wrong. If so, admit it and get on with the interview.

15) Do not dwell at length on your present job

The opening question may relate to your present assignment. Answer the question but do not go into an extended discussion. You are being examined for a *new* job, not your present one. As a matter of fact, try to phrase ALL your answers in terms of the job for which you are being examined.

Basis of Rating

Probably you will forget most of these "do's" and "don'ts" when you walk into the oral interview room. Even remembering them all will not ensure you a passing grade. Perhaps you did not have the qualifications in the first place. But remembering them will help you to put your best foot forward, without treading on the toes of the board members.

Rumor and popular opinion to the contrary notwithstanding, an oral board wants you to make the best appearance possible. They know you are under pressure – but they also want to see how you respond to it as a guide to what your reaction would be under the pressures of the job you seek. They will be influenced by the degree of poise you display, the personal traits you show and the manner in which you respond.

ABOUT THIS BOOK

This book contains tests divided into Examination Sections. Go through each test, answering every question in the margin. At the end of each test look at the answer key and check your answers. On the ones you got wrong, look at the right answer choice and learn. Do not fill in the answers first. Do not memorize the questions and answers, but understand the answer and principles involved. On your test, the questions will likely be different from the samples. Questions are changed and new ones added. If you understand these past questions you should have success with any changes that arise. Tests may consist of several types of questions. We have additional books on each subject should more study be advisable or necessary for you. Finally, the more you study, the better prepared you will be. This book is intended to be the last thing you study before you walk into the examination room. Prior study of relevant texts is also recommended. NLC publishes some of these in our Fundamental Series. Knowledge and good sense are important factors in passing your exam. Good luck also helps. So now study this Passbook, absorb the material contained within and take that knowledge into the examination. Then do your best to pass that exam.

———

EXAMINATION SECTION

EXAMINATION SECTION

TEST 1

DIRECTIONS: Each question or incomplete statement is followed by several suggested answers or completions. Select the one that BEST answers the question or completes the statement. *PRINT THE LETTER OF THE CORRECT ANSWER IN THE SPACE AT THE RIGHT.*

Questions 1-5.

DIRECTIONS: Arrange the following names in alphabetical order as they would appear on the hold shelf of a library by matching the name in Column A with its order position in Column B.

Column A	Column B	
1. Smiles, Roy	A. First	1.____
	B. Second	
2. Smigel, Robert	C. Third	2.____
	D. Fourth	
3. Smith, Raymond	E. Fifth	3.____
4. Smith, Rhonda		4.____
5. Smiegel, Rayna		5.____

Questions 6-10.

DIRECTIONS: Each of Questions 6 through 10 may be:
A. Incorrect due to improper spelling
B. Incorrect due to improper punctuation
C. Incorrect due to improper capitalization
D. Correct

6. The reference section is non-circulating, this means you can't check these items out. 6.____

7. The book can be found in the non-ficton section of the library. 7.____

8. Biographies are a popular selection among all age groups at our library. 8.____

9. The elm grove library is the third biggest library in the county. 9.____

10. Since your book was one week overdue, I cannot wave this fine for you. 10.____

Questions 11-15.

DIRECTIONS: Questions 11 through 15 are to be answered SOLELY on the basis of the information given in the following paragraph.

Libraries have a long history, with the oldest recorded library dating back to Ancient Egypt circa 367 BC to 283 BC. In recent years, however, technological developments have changed the nature of library service. The rise of the internet and the growing number of digital libraries have resulted in a decrease in library usage. Throughout history, library service has primarily focused on the collection of books and other resources a library offers to its patrons. This collection-centered approach to library service has been challenged by the public's ability to access much of this information virtually without ever stepping inside of a library. Fortunately, there is another approach to library service that remains useful and relevant in the digital age: a user-centered approach. A user-centered approach shifts the focus from a library's physical collection to the services it provides to promote learning and social interaction among its users.

11.   Based on what you've read in the above paragraph, which of the following   11._____
        would be an example of user-centered library service?
        A.   A library's acquisition of a rare manuscript
        B.   The expansion of a library's digital collection
        C.   The installation of more shelving to house a larger and more diverse
              collection
        D.   the creation of a librarian-led study group for adult learners returning to
              school

12.   According to the above paragraph, libraries have been around for about _____   12._____
        years.
        A.   500   B.   2,300   C.   1,700   D.   100

13.   According to the above paragraph, what has made a collection-centered   13._____
        approach to library service less useful?
        A.   Poor collection development   B.   A decrease in book prices
        C.   Technological advancements   D.   A more educated public

14.   Based on what you've read in the above paragraph, what must libraries   14._____
        do to remain relevant in the modern age?
        A.   Adopt a user-centered approach to library service
        B.   Adopt a collection-centered approach to library service
        C.   Seek funding from new sources
        D.   Abandon physical collections for completely digital collections

15.   Based on what you've read in the above paragraph, which of the following   15._____
        BEST describes the difference between collection-centered and user-centered
        library service?
        Collection-centered library service focuses on _____, while user-centered
        library service focuses on _____.
        A.   the services a library offers that promote learning and socialization; a
              library's physical holdings of books and resources
        B.   digitizing a library's entire collection; maintaining a physical collection

C. maintaining a physical collection; digitizing a library's entire collection
D. a library's physical holdings of books and resources; the services a library offers that promote learning and socialization

Questions 16-20.

DIRECTIONS: Questions 16 through 20 each consist of four call numbers in Column A and Column B. Compare the numbers listed in each column and use the following to provide your answer:
A. One call number in Column A and Column B are the same
B. Two call numbers in Column A and Column B are the same
C. Three call numbers in Column A and Column B are the same
D. All four call numbers in Column A and Column B are the same

	Column A	Column B	
16.	696.45 BAC	696.45 CAB	16._____
	645.96 CAB	645.96 BAC	
	656.46 DAN	656.46 DAN	
	646.56 AND	646.56 AND	
17.	251.84 NEJ	251.84 NEJ	17._____
	258.14 ENE	258.14 ENE	
	284.84 NEE	284.84 NEE	
	248.15 JEE	248.15 JEE	
18.	199.33 WEN	199.33 WEN	18._____
	139.93 WEW	139.93 WEN	
	113.31 NEW	113.31 WEW	
	133.99 WEE	133.93 WEE	
19.	823.65 HOW	823.65 HOW	19._____
	832.56 WHO	823.56 WHO	
	862.35 WOW	862.35 WOW	
	856.23 WON	856.23 WON	
20.	429.55 BEB	429.55 BEB	20._____
	495.22 BEE	492.22 BEE	
	422.95 EBB	422.95 EBB	
	492.59 EBE	495.29 EBE	

Questions 21-25.

DIRECTIONS: Questions 21 through 25 are to be answered on the basis of the following table.

Dry Creek Library Monthly Adult Program Records				
Program	Number of Attendees Ages 18-24	Number of Attendees Ages 25-44	Number of Attendees Ages 45-65	Number of Attendees Age 65+
Writers' Group	4	5	4	3
Knitting Circle	4	3	3	2
Tai Chi	3	4	1	6
Mystery Book Club	0	2	3	4
Non-Fiction Book Club	2	5	4	3

21. Which program has the HIGHEST attendance rate?   21.____
    A. Writers' Group   B. Tai Chi
    C. Non-Fiction Book Club   D. Knitting Circle

22. Which age group has the HIGHEST participation rate in monthly library   22.____
programs?
    A. 18-24   B. 25-44   C. 45-65   D. 65+

23. Which program is MOST popular among 18 to 44 year olds?   23.____
    A. Writers' Group   B. Knitting Club
    C. Mystery Book Club   D. Non-Fiction Book Club

24. If the library were to discontinue a program, which program would be the   24.____
MOST logical choice based upon these program records?
    A. Writers' Group   B. Tai Chi
    C. Mystery Book Club   D. Knitting Circle

25. If the library wants to expand one program from monthly to weekly in   25.____
order to attract more seniors, which program would be the MOST logical choice
based on these program records?
    A. Writers' Group   B. Knitting Circle
    C. Mystery Book Club   D. Tai Chi

KEY (CORRECT ANSWERS)

1.	C		11.	D
2.	B		12.	B
3.	D		13.	C
4.	E		14.	A
5.	A		15.	D
6.	B		16.	B
7.	A		17.	D
8.	D		18.	A
9.	C		19.	C
10.	A		20.	B

21.	A
22.	B
23.	A
24.	C
25.	D

———

TEST 2

DIRECTIONS: Each question or incomplete statement is followed by several suggested answers or completions. Select the one that BEST answers the question or completes the statement. *PRINT THE LETTER OF THE CORRECT ANSWER IN THE SPACE AT THE RIGHT.*

1. Which of the following words is spelled INCORRECTLY?   1.____
   A. microfiche   B. photocopyer   C. interlibrary   D. catalog

2. Which of the following sentences includes an error in punctuation?   2.____
   A. I'm holding Mr. Rutgers book at the circulation desk.
   B. All meeting rooms are currently reserved.
   C. Only library cardholders can request books through interlibrary loan.
   D. Children's books are located upstairs in the Youth Services Department.

3. Which of the following sentences includes a capitalization error?   3.____
   A. The library director must sign off on all purchases.
   B. This week the Ashton Public Library Book Club is reading *The Paris Wife*.
   C. If you need help with academic research, you should speak with a librarian in the reference department.
   D. Our most popular program is our weekly Gourmet Club, where people come together to talk about fine food and drinks.

4. Which of the following words is spelled INCORRECTLY?   4.____
   A. biography   B. anthology   C. magizine   D. bibliography

5. Which of the following sentences includes an error in punctuation?   5.____
   A. Can I see your driver's license?
   B. Ms Janda said that she would be arriving 10 minutes late for the computer class.
   C. There are only three copies left of the book selected for the monthly book club.
   D. Who did you speak to over the phone about this hold request.

Questions 6-10.

DIRECTIONS: Questions 6 through 10 include sentences with one word underlined. For each question, please select the word with the CLOSEST meaning to the underlined word.

6. Mr. Banks has a block on his account because he has too many <u>fines</u>.   6.____
   A. charges   B. items   C. warnings   D. restrictions

7. *The Girl With the Dragon Tattoo* received overwhelmingly positive <u>reviews</u>.   7.____
   A. investments   B. reassessments
   C. critiques   D. inspections

8. When you write a research paper, you must include <u>citations</u>.   8.____
    A. commendations   B. references
    C. facts   D. inferences

9. If you make a copy of that CD, you are <u>infringing</u> upon copyright law.   9.____
    A. preserving   B. misunderstanding
    C. violating   D. elucidating

10. *Architectural Digest* is located on the first floor with the other <u>serials</u>.   10.____
    A. books   B. databases   C. periodicals   D. archives

Questions 11-15.

DIRECTIONS: Questions 11 through 15 consist of four addresses in Column A and Column B. Compare the addresses listed in each column and use the following to provide your answer:
    A. One address in Column A and Column B are the same.
    B. Two addresses in Column A and Column B are the same.
    C. Three addresses in Column A and Column B are the same.
    D. All four addresses in Column A and Column B are the same.

<u>Column A</u>

<u>Column B</u>

11. 3941 Blackwell Dr.   3941 Blackwell Dr.   11.____
     3491 Blackwell Dr.   3914 Balckwell Dr.
     3991 Blackswell St.   3941 Blackwell St.
     3945 Blackstreet Ave.   3945 Blackstreet Dr.

12. 204 Rhodes Ave. Apt. B   204 Rhodes Ave. Apt. B   12.____
     206 Rhodes Ave. Apt. 6   204 Rhodes Ave. Apt 4
     206 Rhoades Ave. Apt B   206 Rhoades Ave. Apt. B
     260 Rhodes St. Apt. B6   260 Rhodes St. Apt. B6

13. 1155 Judith Rd.   1155 Judith Rd.   13.____
     1515 Judith Ln.   1515 Judith Ln.
     5111 Judy Rd.   5111 Judy Rd.
     1155 Judy Ln.   1155 Judy Ln.

14. 2367 Cascade Blvd.   2376 Cascade Blvd.   14.____
     7632 Cascade Ave.   7632 Cascade Ave.
     2367 Cascadia Blvd.   2367 Cascadia Blvd.
     7632 Cascade Blvd.   7632 Cascadia Blvd.

15. 106 Brooks Ln. Apt. 12   106 Brooks Ln. Apt. 12   15.____
     102 Brooks Ln. Apt. 16   102 Brooks Ln. Apt. 16
     126 Brook Ln. Apt. 11   126 Brooks Ln. Apt. 11
     162 Brook Ave. Apt. 2   166 Brook Ave. Apt. 2

Questions 16-20.

DIRECTIONS: In Questions 16 through 20, please match the author's last name in Column A
with its proper order on the shelf of a library that organizes fiction alphabetically
by author's last name in Column B.

Column A   Column B

16.   Brockenstein   A.   First   16._____
                                      B.   Second
17.   Brock   C.   Third   17._____
                                      D.   Fourth
18.   Broadchurch   E.   Fifth   18._____

19.   Broadbent   19._____

20.   Brockley   20._____

21.   If a patron returns five books two days past their due date, and overdue   21._____
      charges accrue at 15 cents per day for each book, how much does the patron
      owe in overdue fees?
         A. $3.00   B. $1.75   C. $15.00   D. $5.75

22.   Susan is compiling statistics from monthly library usage records. Records   22._____
      state that over the course of one month, patrons checked out 5,375 adult fiction
      titles, 4,789 adult non-fiction titles, 6,854 audio-visual items, and 3, 632
      magazines. Based on these records, fiction titles comprise about _____
      percent of overall monthly circulation.
         A. 52   B. 26   C. 15   D. 38

23.   Yearly statistics show that over the course of one week an average of 33   23._____
      patrons attend library programs. If there are four programs scheduled during
      one week, about how many patrons will be attending each program?
         A. 3   B. 11   C. 5   D. 8

24.   Jane is calling patrons to inform them that the interlibrary loan books they   24._____
      requested have arrived. It takes Jane approximately five minutes to notify each
      patron, and she has a cart filled with 37 interlibrary books that require patron
      notification. She also has a bin full of returned books that need to be checked
      in and shelved. How long will it take Jane to finish the hold notifications so she
      can move on to her next task?
         A. One hour   B. About six hours
         C. About three hours   D. 45 minutes

25. Birch Grove Library has a rule that patrons can only check out 50 books at a time, 50 audio-visual items at a time, and 15 interlibrary loan items at a time. The library also has a rule that no more than 75 items total can be checked out to a patron's account at one time. If a patron already has 45 books, 25 audio-visual items, and 5 interlibrary loan items checked out, she can
    25._____
    A. still check out 5 books, 25 audio-visual items, 5 interlibrary loan items
    B. no longer check anything out until she returns some of her items
    C. still check out 30 books
    D. still check out 10 interlibrary loan items and 25 audio-visual items

---

KEY (CORRECT ANSWERS)

1.	B		11.	A
2.	A		12.	C
3.	C		13.	D
4.	C		14.	B
5.	D		15.	B
6.	A		16.	D
7.	C		17.	C
8.	B		18.	B
9.	C		19.	A
10.	C		20.	E

21.	A
22.	B
23.	D
24.	C
25.	B

TEST 3

DIRECTIONS: Each question or incomplete statement is followed by several suggested answers or completions. Select the one that BEST answers the question or completes the statement. *PRINT THE LETTER OF THE CORRECT ANSWER IN THE SPACE AT THE RIGHT.*

Questions 1-5.

DIRECTIONS: Questions 1 through 5 are to be answered on the basis of the following paragraph.

Copyright law plays an important role in how libraries operate and provide information to their patrons. Libraries must abide by state and federal copyright laws, including the Copyright Act, which is the most authoritative source of copyright law in the United States. Through the Copyright Act's first sale doctrine, libraries are allowed to lend books and other copyrighted material. Additionally, the Copyright Act's fair use law allows library patrons to use copyrighted materials for specific functions, such as criticism, comment, news reporting, scholarship, and research. Copyright law also allows libraries to reproduce copyrighted works in order to preserve or replace these works or provide them to people with disabilities.

1. Which of the following would NOT be an acceptable reason for a library to reproduce copyrighted material? 1.____
   A. To deliver it to a person who is housebound due to a physical disability
   B. To sell it in the library's book sale in order to raise funds for the library's remodel
   C. To preserve a book that is currently out of print and that also has limited used copies available
   D. To replace a copy of a rare book that has been lost

2. Which law allows libraries to lend books and other copyrighted materials? 2.____
   A. This is not allowed under state or federal law
   B. The fair use law
   C. The first sale doctrine
   D. The first use act

3. Based on the fair use law, libraries can allow patrons to quote or use passages from copyrighted materials in 3.____
   A. newspaper articles
   B. business brochures
   C. book manuscripts set for publication
   D. television advertisements

4. In the United States, copyright law PRIMARILY comes from 4.____
   A. state law   B. the first use act
   C. municipal law   D. the Copyright Act

5. The fair use law can be found in   5.____
    A. state law   B. the Copyright Act
    C. the First Amendment   D. municipal law

6. Which of the following words is spelled INCORRECTLY?   6.____
    A. alamnac   B. dictionary   C. atlas   D. encyclopedia

7. Which of the following sentences contains an error in punctuation?   7.____
    A. There are two titles on hold for members of the library's book club: *Gone Girl* and *Me Before You.*
    B. At the beginning of each month the library director holds a staff meeting that everyone is required to attend.
    C. Did you ask the patron for her photo I.D. before providing her with her account information?
    D. The library's Knitting Circle meets the first Thursday, second Saturday and third Monday of every month.

8. Which of the following words is spelled INCORRECTLY?   8.____
    A. classification   B. plagarism   C. withdrawn   D. volume

9. Which of the following sentences includes an error in capitalization?   9.____
    A. All of the items you had on hold were sent back Tuesday.
    B. Did Mr. Phekos register for this week's cooking demonstration?
    C. Tanner is helping with the fundraiser because he is a member of the friends of the library.
    D. Book donations can be placed in the donation box near the circulation desk.

10. Which of the following words is spelled INCORRECTLY?   10.____
    A. thesarus   B. thesis   C. series   D. reserve

Questions 11-15.

DIRECTIONS: Questions 11 through 15 each contain three lines of letters in Column A and three lines of numbers in Column B. The letters in each line should correspond with the numbers in each line as outlined in the following table:

Letter	J	R	D	T	M	C	P	K	O	S
Matching Number	0	1	2	3	4	5	6	7	8	9

Please answer the questions as follows:
A. None of the lines of letters and lines of numbers are matched correctly.
B. One of the lines of letters and numbers is matched correctly.
C. Two of the lines of letters and lines of numbers are matched correctly.
D. All three of the lines of letters and lines of numbers are matched correctly.

	Column A	Column B	
11.	JMCP	0456	11.____
	RMKS	1479	
	CPRO	5618	
12.	DRKS	9172	12.____
	MKPJ	4761	
	JDCP	0256	
13.	CSDJ	5924	13.____
	RKRD	1712	
	JKPC	0765	
14.	TMMO	3448	14.____
	CPDR	5632	
	JOTS	0839	
15.	JCMS	0648	15.____
	ROST	1983	
	MKJD	4701	

Questions 16-20.

DIRECTIONS: In Questions 16 through 20, match the book title in Column A with its proper alphabetical orders based on letter by letter filing rules.

	Column A	Column B	
16.	To Kill a Mockingbird	A. First	16.____
		B. Second	
17.	A Tale of Two Cities	C. Third	17.____
		D. Fourth	
18.	The Time Traveler's Wife	E. Fifth	18.____
19.	Treasure Island		19.____
20.	The Two Towers		20.____

Questions 21-25.

DIRECTIONS: Questions 21 through 25 are to be answered on the basis of the following table.

Dry Creek Library 2015 Library Card Registration by Season					
Season	Number of Registrants Under 18	Number of Registrants Ages 18-24	Number of Registrants Ages 25-44	Number of Registrants Ages 45-65	Number of Registrants Age 65+
Winter	56	34	69	48	34
Spring	72	47	55	62	48
Summer	100	75	71	89	101
Fall	96	115	88	72	63

21. During which season does Dry Creek Library experience the MOST library card registrations?
    A. Winter   B. Spring   C. Summer   D. Fall

21.____

22. Which of the following age groups registered for the MOST library cards in 2015?
    A. Under 18   B. 18-24   C. 25-44   D. 45-65

22.____

23. Which of the following patrons is MOST likely to register for a library card in the fall based on the data shown in the above table?
    A. A 10-year-old preparing for the new school year
    B. A 65-year-old who has just retired from his full-time job
    C. An 18-year-old entering her first semester of college
    D. A 26-year-old enrolled in medical school

23.____

24. During which season should Dry Creek Library increase marketing efforts to draw in more registrants between the ages of 18 and 24?
    A. Winter   B. Spring   C. Summer   D. Fall

24.____

25. In 2014, 1,364 people registered for new library cards. How does this number compare to the number of registrants in 2015?
It is _____ registered in 2015.
    A. the same amount of people that
    B. slightly less than the number of people who
    C. significantly more than the number of people who
    D. significantly less than the number of people who

25.____

KEY (CORRECT ANSWERS)

1.	B		11.	D
2.	C		12.	B
3.	A		13.	C
4.	D		14.	C
5.	B		15.	A
6.	A		16.	C
7.	B		17.	A
8.	B		18.	B
9.	C		19.	D
10.	A		20.	E

21.	C
22.	A
23.	C
24.	A
25.	B

———————

TEST 4

DIRECTIONS: Each question or incomplete statement is followed by several suggested answers or completions. Select the one that BEST answers the question or completes the statement. *PRINT THE LETTER OF THE CORRECT ANSWER IN THE SPACE AT THE RIGHT.*

Questions 1-5.

DIRECTIONS: Each of the sentences provided in Questions 1 through 5 may be:
A. Incorrect due to improper spelling
B. Incorrect due to improper punctuation
C. Incorrect due to improper capitalization
D. Correct

1. When you search the library's catalog online you can search by author, title, subject or, keyword.   1.____

2. The movie "Ghostbusters" is available on DVD or Blu-Ray in the library's audiovisual department.   2.____

3. The library hosts a group for writers that meets monthly and a children's story hour that meets weekly.   3.____

4. Reference librarians are best equipped to answer questions about the library's electronic resorces.   4.____

5. Library patrons can sign into their library account online to pay fines, rezerve books and check their due dates.   5.____

Questions 6-10.

DIRECTIONS: Questions 6 through 10 include sentences with one word underlined. Please select the word with the CLOSEST meaning to the underlined word.

6. The patron has <u>requested</u> that the book be held for an extra two days because she is on vacation.   6.____
   A. refused   B. asked   C. determined   D. stated

7. The Oak Creek Village Library participates in a <u>reciprocal</u> borrowing program in which it shares library materials with 25 other libraries.   7.____
   A. individual   B. restrictive
   C. collaborative   D. bibliographic

8. In libraries, books are assigned a call number based upon the book's <u>subject</u>.   8.____
   A. title   B. author   C. chronology   D. topic

9. Every year, the library director and board of directors review and update   9.____
   library <u>policies</u>.
     A. procedures   B. collections   C. events   D. affairs

10. Librarians at the Poplar Lane Library are sometimes asked to <u>proctor</u> official   10.____
    tests and exams.
      A. barter   B. supervise   C. process   D. create

Questions 11-15.

DIRECTIONS: In answering Questions 11 through 15, arrange the following names in
              alphabetical order as they would appear on the hold shelf of a library by
              matching the name in Column A with its order position in Column B.

      Column A   Column B

11. Frey, James   A. First   11.____
                                      B. Second
12. Friend, Jayne   C. Third   12.____
                                      D. Fourth
13. Frye, Jada   E. Fifth   13.____

14. Friel, Jewel   14.____

15. Frillo, Juno   15.____

Questions 16-20.

DIRECTIONS: Questions 16 through 20 each consist of four call numbers in Column A and
              Column B. Compare the numbers listed in each column and use the following
              to provide your answer:
              A. One call number in Column A and Column B are the same.
              B. Two call numbers in Column A and Column B are the same.
              C. Three call numbers in Column A and Column B are the same.
              D. All four call numbers in Column A and Column B are the same.

      Column A   Column B

16. 147.74CAL   147.74CAL   16.____
     174.47LAC   174.44LAC
     144.77LAL   177.44LAL
     411.77CAC   477.11CAL

17. 467.09DAN   467.09DAN   17.____
     469.07DAD   469.07DAD
     460.79NAD   460.79NAD
     468.32DAJ   468.23DAJ

18.
219.57KAR	219.57KAR
215.97KAR	215.57KAR
257.19RAR	257.19RAR
275.19KAK	275.19KAK

18.____

19.
112.48PAU	112.58PAU
112.85PUA	112.85PUA
124.18PUL	124.18PUL
142.85PAU	142.85PAA

19.____

20.
102.75CHR	102.75CHR
175.27CRI	175.27CRI
107.25CHR	107.25CHR
157.22CRI	157.22CRI

20.____

21. Old Towne Library is hosting a speaking event and book signing with a well-known author. Seats are available for 120 people, but the author only has one hour to sign books afterward. If it takes about three minutes to sign each person's book, how many of the event's attendees will be able to participate in the book signing?

    A. All of them   B. 20   C. 100   D. 50

21.____

22. If Fleetwood Library owns a total of 1,000 DVDs (500 in the fiction section and 500 in the non-fiction section), how many DVDs would the library have left if the library director decided to withdraw 120 fiction DVDs and 150 non-fiction DVDs, while simultaneously adding 75 fiction DVDs and 60 non-fiction DVDs?

    A. 730   B. 805   C. 865   D. 950

22.____

23. Tandy has been asked to create the schedule for the circulation staff at Morton Pass Library. The library is open from 10 A.M. to 9 P.M. Monday through Friday, from 10 A.M. to 5 P.M. on Saturday, and from 12 P.M. to 5 P.M. on Sunday. The library director requires that two staff members work at the desk during all hours of operation. What is the TOTAL number of hours Tandy will need to schedule staff for next week's schedule?

    A. 134   B. 55   C. 201   D. 68

23.____

24. The Boynton Canyon Library hosts a weekly book discussion group every Thursday night. If 8 people attended the group the first week of February, 11 attended the second week, 7 attended the third week, and 10 attended the fourth week, what is the average number of attendees for the month of February?

    A. 9   B. 34   C. 10   D. 7

24.____

25. A library patron has $6.60 in fines on his library account. He returns five more books five days late and is charged $.15 a day for each book. The library does not let patrons check out library materials when the fines on their account exceed $10.00. Which of the following statements BEST describes the patron's current situation?

The patron

   A. has less than $10.00 in fines and can still check out library materials
   B. must pay at least $1.00 in fines before he can check out more library materials
   C. must pay at least $.60 in fines before he can check out more library materials
   D. must pay at least $.35 in fines before he can check out more library materials

25.____

_____

KEY (CORRECT ANSWERS)

1.	B		11.	A
2.	C		12.	C
3.	D		13.	E
4.	A		14.	B
5.	A		15.	D
6.	B		16.	A
7.	C		17.	C
8.	D		18.	C
9.	A		19.	B
10.	B		20.	D

21.	B
22.	C
23.	A
24.	A
25.	D

EXAMINATION SECTION
TEST 1

DIRECTIONS: Each question or incomplete statement is followed by several suggested answers or completions. Select the one that BEST answers the question or completes the statement. *PRINT THE LETTER OF THE CORRECT ANSWER IN THE SPACE AT THE RIGHT.*

1. A book about the life of another person is called a(n)   1._____

   A. monograph   B. fiction   C. biography
   D. autobiography   E. reference

2. A book about real experiences is usually referred to as a(n)   2._____

   A. reference   B. monograph   C. fiction
   D. non-fiction   E. autobiography

3. The Dewey Decimal system is a   3._____

   A. list of books, magazines, and non-print materials
   B. system for checking out books
   C. method for organizing materials
   D. system for filing cards
   E. system for networking

4. A catalog card reading MOVIE see MOTION PICTURE means: 4._____

   A. All books on movies will be found under the subject heading MOTION PICTURE
   B. Additional books on movies will be found under the subject heading MOTION PIC-TURE
   C. Another library has the motion picture holdings
   D. Materials are expected on motion pictures
   E. All materials on movies are circulating

5. A bibliography is a(n)   5._____

   A. encyclopedia   B. networking
   C. means of circulating materials D. list of materials
   E. reference tool

6. An annotation is a(n)   6._____

   A. review   B. explanatory note   C. precis
   D. format   E. critique

7. AMERICAN REFERENCE BOOKS ANNUAL provides a   7._____

   A. comprehensive reviewing service of reference books published in the United States
   B. monthly periodical furnishing reviews of popular reference tools
   C. publisher's guide to monthly reviewing sources
   D. professional journal published by the American Library Association
   E. bibliography of bibliographies

8. An index is a(n)   8.____

    A. table of contents   B. encyclopedia
    C. series of footnotes   D. bibliography
    E. guide to locate material

9. The library catalog is a(n)   9.____

    A. shelf list
    B. index to the materials collection
    C. bibliography
    D. system for reserves
    E. collection of book orders

10. A shelf list is a   10.____

    A. record of materials in a library
    B. reserve list
    C. weeding list
    D. list of reference materials
    E. bibliography of reference sources

11. Technical services include   11.____

    A. acquisitions, cataloging, and materials preparation
    B. reference work and user services
    C. reader's advisory services
    D. circulation and reference services
    E. networking

12. A collection of materials such as pamphlets, clippings, or illustrations kept in special con- 12.____
tainers is referred to as a

    A. card catalog   B. card file   C. vertical file
    D. container collection   E. clipping file

13. An electromagnetic recording made for playback on a television set is referred to as a(n)   13.____

    A. audio tape   B. cassette   C. video-recording
    D. superdisk   E. fiche

14. A word, name, object, group of words, or acronym describing a subject is usually referred   14.____
to as a

    A. cross reference   B. subject heading
    C. nom de plume   D. serial
    E. catalog card

15. A collection of materials with restricted circulation usually found in college and university 15.____
libraries is called a(n) _____ collection.

    A. reserved materials   B. patron   C. student
    D. open stack   E. rotating reserve

16. An independent publication of forty-nine pages or less, bound in paper covers, is called a   16.____

    A. serial   B. monograph   C. microcard
    D. pamphlet   E. fiche

17. Library work directly concerned with assistance to readers in securing information and in using library resources is termed

    17._____

  A. circulation services   B. technical services
  C. reader's advisory services   D. user services
  E. networking

18. A three-dimensional representation of a real object reproduced in the original size or to scale is called a(n)

    18._____

  A. model   B. film   C. microform
  D. ultrafiche   E. videotape

19. The act of filling out required forms to become an eligible library borrower is called

    19._____

  A. serialization   B. direction   C. registration
  D. reference work   E. signing

20. A direction in a catalog that guides the user to related names or subjects is termed a _____ reference.

    20._____

  A. shelf   B. see-also   C. title
  D. see   E. subject

21. A record of a work in the catalog under the title is called a

    21._____

  A. subject card   B. number entry   C. author card
  D. subject entry   E. title entry

22. The printed scheme of a classification system is referred to as a

    22._____

  A. classification schedule   B. numbering schedule
  C. lettering schedule   D. cutter number
  E. copyright

23. The entry of a work in the catalog under the subject heading is called a

    23._____

  A. subject card   B. subject heading   C. subject entry
  D. reference entry   E. subject guide

24. The department in a library responsible for officially listing prospective borrowers is the _____ department.

    24._____

  A. reference   B. registration   C. welcoming
  D. circulation   E. technical

25. Library work that deals with patrons and the use of the library collection is called _____ services.

    25._____

  A. technical   B. reader   C. circulation
  D. reference   E. public

KEY (CORRECT ANSWERS)

1.	C		11.	A
2.	D		12.	C
3.	C		13.	C
4.	A		14.	B
5.	D		15.	A
6.	B		16.	D
7.	A		17.	D
8.	E		18.	A
9.	B		19.	C
10.	A		20.	B

21.	E
22.	A
23.	C
24.	B
25.	D

TEST 2

DIRECTIONS: Each question or incomplete statement is followed by several suggested answers or completions. Select the one that BEST answers the question or completes the statement. *PRINT THE LETTER OF THE CORRECT ANSWER IN THE SPACE AT THE RIGHT.*

1. Material held for a borrower for a limited time is termed _____ material.   1._____

    A. reference   B. reserved   C. circulation
    D. special   E. held

2. A notice sent to a borrower to remind him to return heldover due material is a(n)   2._____

    A. warning   B. notice   C. overdue notice
    D. warning notice   E. call slip

3. Material returned to the library before the date due is   3._____

    A. Penalized   B. returned   C. accepted
    D. unneeded   E. subject to examination

4. Real objects, specimens, or artifacts are called   4._____

    A. toys   B. realia   C. games
    D. opaque material   E. models

5. A film with a series of pictures in sequence which creates the illusion of motion when projected is classified as a   5._____

    A. photogram   B. motion picture   C. videotape
    D. cassette   E. slide

6. Laying books on the shelves in proper order is called   6._____

    A. placing   B. weeding   C. reading   D. shifting   E. shelving

7. A publication issued in successive parts usually to be continued indefinitely is referred to as a   7._____

    A. paper   B. monograph C. serial   D. pamphlet   E. edition

8. A record of the loan of material is called a   8._____

    A. call slip   B. reserve   C. contract   D. copy   E. charge

9. Information arranged in tabular, outline, or graphic form on a sheet of paper is called a   9._____

    A. classification   B. charge   C. chart
    D. catalog   E. cartoon

10. The method used to lend materials to borrowers and maintain the necessary records is the _____ system.   10._____

    A. classification   B. circulation control   C. reference
    D. borrowing   E. returnable

11. Any entry, other than a subject entry, that is made in a catalog in addition to the main entry is called a(n)   11.____

    A. added entry   B. call number   C. central reference
    D. reference entry   E. explanatory entry

12. The record of the number of items charged out of a library is termed   12.____

    A. record statistics   B. circulation statistics
    C. circulation control   D. record control
    E. itemizing

13. A number assigned to each book or item as it is received by the library is referred to as a(n) _____ number.   13.____

    A. call   B. accession   C. entry
    D. acquisition   E. ordering

14. A master file of all registered borrowers in a library system is called the _____ file.   14.____

    A. personnel   B. charging   C. classification
    D. central registration   E. circulation control

15. A person who charges out materials from a library is called the   15.____

    A. lender   B. technician   C. professional librarian
    D. clerk   E. borrower

16. A catalog in which all entries are filed in alphabetical order is called a(n) _____ catalog.   16.____

    A. card   B. Library of Congress   C. alphabetical
    D. dictionary   E. subject

17. The day material is to be returned to a library is usually referred to as the _____ day.   17.____

    A. library   B. date-due   C. return
    D. book   E. library-due

18. The act of annulling the library's record of a loan is called   18.____

    A. discharging   B. cancelling   C. stamping
    D. recording   E. unloaning

19. The penalty charge for material returned after the date due is called a(n)   19.____

    A. charge   B. fine   C. tax   D. levy   E. arrangement

20. A set of materials containing rules designed to be played in a competitive situation is called a   20.____

    A. rolodome   B. game   C. sketch   D. linedex   E. materialsset

21. A catalog in more than one part is termed a _____ catalog.   21.____

    A. divided   B. split   C. Library of Congress
    D. Dewey   E. Sears

22. A metal file containing a number of flat metal leaves that hold single cardboard strips list-   22.____
ing titles and holdings is called a

    A.   linedesk   B.   linetop   C.   rolotop
    D.   rotofile   E.   linedex

23. A metal file containing a number of shallow drawers in which serial check-in cards are   23.____
kept is usually referred to as a

    A.   linedesk   B.   rotofile   C.   box   D.   kardex   E.   linetop

24. The strip of paper pasted in the book or on the book packet, on which the date due is   24.____
stamped, is called the

    A.   date slip   B.   date card   C.   date strip
    D.   call slip   E.   card strip

25. Film on which materials have been photographed in greatly reduced size is called   25.____

    A.   minifilm   B.   microfilm   C.   photogram
    D.   miniaturization   E.   photoreduction

KEY (CORRECT ANSWERS)

1.	B		11.	A
2.	C		12.	B
3.	C		13.	B
4.	B		14.	D
5.	B		15.	E
6.	E		16.	D
7.	C		17.	B
8.	E		18.	A
9.	C		19.	B
10.	B		20.	B

21.	A
22.	E
23.	D
24.	A
25.	B

EXAMINATION SECTION
TEST 1

DIRECTIONS: Each question or incomplete statement is followed by several suggested answers or completions. Select the one that *BEST* answers the question or completes the statement. *PRINT THE LETTER OF THE CORRECT ANSWER IN THE SPACE AT THE RIGHT.*

Questions 1-5.

DIRECTIONS: Each question from 1 to 5 consists of a sentence with an underlined word. For each question, select the choice that is *CLOSEST* in meaning to the underlined word.

EXAMPLE

This division reviews the <u>fiscal</u> reports of the agency.
In this sentence the word *fiscal* means most nearly
  A. financial   B. critical   C. basic   D. personnel
The correct answer is A. "financial" because "financial" is closest to *fiscal*. Therefore, the answer is A.

1. Every good office worker needs <u>basic</u> skills.   1._____
    The word *basic* in this sentence means

    A. fundamental   B. advanced   C. unusual   D. outstanding

2. He turned out to be a good <u>instructor</u>.   2._____
    The word *instructor* in this sentence means

    A. student   B. worker   C. typist   D. teacher

3. The <u>quantity</u> of work in the office was under study.   3._____
    In this sentence, the word *quantity* means

    A. amount   B. flow   C. supervision   D. type

4. The morning was spent <u>examining</u> the time records.   4._____
    In this sentence, the word *examining* means

    A. distributing   B. collecting   C. checking   D. filing

5. The candidate filled in the <u>proper</u> spaces on the form.   5._____
    In this sentence, the word *proper* means

    A. blank   B. appropriate   C. many   D. remaining

Questions 6-8.

DIRECTIONS: You are to answer Questions 6 through 8 *SOLELY* on the basis of the information contained in the following paragraph:

The increase in the number of public documents in the last two centuries closely matches the increase in population in the United States. The great number of public documents has become a serious threat to their usefulness. It is necessary to have programs which will reduce the number of public documents that are kept and which will, at the same time, assure keeping those that have value. Such programs need a great deal of thought to have any success.

6. According to the above paragraph, public documents may be less useful if   6._____

    A. the files are open to the public
    B. the record room is too small
    C. the copying machine is operated only during normal working hours
    D. too many records are being kept

7. According to the above paragraph, the growth of the population in the United States has   7._____
matched the growth in the quantity of public documents for a period of, most nearly,

    A. 50 years   B. 100 years   C. 200 years   D. 300 years

8. According to the above paragraph, the increased number of public documents has made   8._____
it necessary to

    A. find out which public documents are worth keeping
    B. reduce the great number of public documents by decreasing government services
    C. eliminate the copying of all original public documents
    D. avoid all new copying devices.

Questions 9-10.

DIRECTIONS: You are to answer Questions 9 and 10 *SOLELY* on the basis of the information
contained in the following paragraph:

The work goals of an agency can best be reached if the employees understand and agree
with these goals. One way to gain such understanding and agreement is for management to
encourage and seriously consider suggestions from employees in the setting of agency goals.

9. On the basis of the paragraph above, the *BEST* way to achieve the work goals of an   9._____
agency is to

    A. make certain that employees work as hard as possible
    B. study the organizational structure of the agency
    C. encourage employees to think seriously about the agency's problems
    D. stimulate employee understanding of the work goals

10. On the basis of the paragraph above, understanding and agreement with agency goals   10._____
can be gained by

    A. allowing the employees to set agency goals
    B. reaching agency goals quickly
    C. legislative review of agency operations
    D. employee participation in setting agency goals

Questions 11-15.

DIRECTIONS: Each of Questions 11 through 15 consists of a group of four words. One word
in each group is *INCORRECTLY* spelled. For each question, print the letter of
the correct answer in the space at the right that is the same as the letter next
to the word which is *INCORRECTLY* spelled.
EXAMPLE
    A. housing   B. certain   C. budgit   D. money

The word "budgit" is incorrectly spelled, because the correct spelling should be "budget." Therefore, the correct answer is C.

11. A. sentince   B. bulletin   C. notice   D. definition   11.____

12. A. appointment   B. exactly   C. typest   D. light   12.____

13. A. penalty   B. suparvise   C. consider   D. division   13.____

14. A. schedule   B. accurate   C. corect   D. simple   14.____

15. A. suggestion   B. installed   C. proper   D. agincy   15.____

Questions 16-20.

DIRECTIONS: Each question from 16 through 20 consists of a sentence which may be
  A. incorrect because of bad word usage, or
  B. incorrect because of bad punctuation, or
  C. incorrect because of bad spelling, or
  D. correct
Read each sentence carefully. Then print in the proper space at the right A, B, C, or D, according to the answer you choose from the four choices listed above. There is only one type of error in each incorrect sentence. If there is no error, the sentence is correct.

EXAMPLE

George Washington was the father of his contry.
This sentence is incorrect because of bad spelling ("contry" instead of "country"). Therefore, the answer is C.

16. The assignment was completed in record time but the payroll for it has not yet been pre-   16.____
     parid.

17. The operator, on the other hand, is willing to learn me how to use the mimeograph.   17.____

18. She is the prettiest of the three sisters.   18.____

19. She doesn't know; if the mail has arrived.   19.____

20. The doorknob of the office door is broke.   20.____

21. A clerk can process a form in 15 minutes. How many forms can that clerk process in six   21.____
     hours?

     A. 10   B. 21   C. 24   D. 90

22. An office staff consists of 120 people. Sixty of them have been assigned to a special   22.____
     project. Of the remaining staff, 20 answer the mail, 10-handle phone calls, and the rest
     operate the office machines. The number of people operating the office machines is

     A. 20   B. 30   C. 40   D. 45

23. An office worker received 65 applications but on the first day had to return 26 of them for   23.____
     being incomplete and on the second day 25 had to be returned for being incomplete.
     How many applications did <u>not</u> have to be returned?

     A. 10   B. 12   C. 14   D. 16

24. An office worker answered 63 phone calls in one day and 91 phone calls the next day. For these 2 days, what was the average number of phone calls he answered per day?

    A. 77   B. 28   C. 82   D. 93

24.____

25. An office worker processed 12 vouchers of $8.75 each, 3 vouchers of $3.68 each, and 2 vouchers of $1.29 each. The total dollar amount of these vouchers is

    A. $116.04   B. $117.52   C. $118.62   D. $119.04

25.____

KEY (CORRECT ANSWERS)

1.	A		11.	A
2.	D		12.	C
3.	A		13.	B
4.	C		14.	C
5.	B		15.	D
6.	D		16.	C
7.	C		17.	A
8.	A		18.	D
9.	D		19.	B
10.	D		20.	A

21.	C
22.	B
23.	C
24.	A
25.	C

TEST 2

DIRECTIONS: Each question or incomplete statement is followed by several suggested answers or completions. Select the one that *BEST* answers the question or completes the statement. *PRINT THE LETTER OF THE CORRECT ANSWER IN THE SPACE AT THE RIGHT.*

Questions 1-5.

DIRECTIONS: Each question from 1 to 5 lists four names. The names may or may not be exactly the same. Compare the names in each question and mark your answer as follows:

Mark your answer A if all the names are different
Mark your answer B if only two names are exactly the same
Mark your answer C if only three names are exactly the same
Mark your answer D if all four names are exactly the same

EXAMPLE

Jensen, Alfred E.
Jensen, Alfred E.
Jensan, Alfred E.
Jensen, Fred E.

Since the name Jensen, Alfred E. appears twice and is exactly the same in both places, the correct answer is B.

1. Riviera, Pedro S.
   Rivers, Pedro S.
   Riviera, Pedro N.
   Riviera, Juan S.   1._____

2. Guider, Albert
   Guidar, Albert
   Giuder, Alfred
   Guider, Albert   2._____

3. Blum, Rona
   Blum, Rona
   Blum, Rona
   Blum, Rona   3._____

4. Raugh, John
   Raugh, James
   Raughe, John
   Raugh, John   4._____

5. Katz, Stanley
   Katz, Stanley
   Katze, Stanley
   Katz, Stanley   5._____

Questions 6-10.

DIRECTIONS: Each Question 6 through 10 consists of numbers or letters in Columns I and II. For each question, compare each line of Column I with its corresponding line in Column II and decide how many lines in Column I are *EXACTLY* the same as their corresponding lines in Column II. In your answer space, mark your answer as follows:

Mark your answer A if only *ONE* line in Column I is exactly the same as its corresponding line in Column II
Mark your answer B if only *TWO* lines in Column I are exactly the same as their corresponding lines in Column II
Mark your answer C if only *THREE* lines in Column I are exactly the same as their corresponding lines in Column II
Mark your answer D if all *FOUR* lines in Column I are exactly the same as their corresponding lines in Column II

EXAMPLE

Column I	Column II
1776	1776
1865	1865
1945	1945
1976	1978

Only three lines in Column I are exactly the same as their corresponding lines in Column II. Therefore, the correct answer is C.

	Column I	Column II	
6.	5653	5653	6.____
	8727	8728	
	ZPSS	ZPSS	
	4952	9453	
7.	PNJP	PNPJ	7.____
	NJPJ	NJPJ	
	JNPN	JNPN	
	PNJP	PNPJ	
8.	effe	eFfe	8.____
	uWvw	uWvw	
	KpGj	KpGg	
	vmnv	vmnv	
9.	5232	5232	9.____
	PfrC	PfrN	
	zssz	zzss	
	rwwr	rwww	
10.	czws	czws	10.____
	cecc	cece	
	thrm	thrm	
	lwtz	lwtz	

Questions 11-15.

DIRECTIONS: Questions 11 through 15 have lines of letters and numbers. Each letter should be matched with its number in accordance with the following table:

Letter	F	R	C	A	W	L	E	N	B	T
Matching Number	0	1	2	3	4	5	6	7	8	9

From the table you can determine that the letter F has the matching number 0 below it, the letter R has the matching number 1 below it, etc.

For each question, compare each line of letters and numbers carefully to see if each letter has its correct matching number. If all the letters and numbers are matched correctly in

none of the lines of the question, mark your answer A

only one of the lines of the question, mark your answer B

only two of the lines of the question, mark your answer C

all three lines of the question, mark your answer D

EXAMPLE

WBCR	4826
TLBF	9580
ATNE	3986

There is a mistake in the first line because the letter R should have its matching number 1 instead of the number 6.

The second line is correct because each letter shown has the correct matching number.

There is a mistake in the third line because the letter N should have the matching number 7 instead of the number 8,

Since all the letters and numbers are matched correctly in only one of the lines in the sample, the correct answer is B.

11. EBCT 6829 11.____
     ATWR 3961
     NLBW 7584

12. RNCT 1729 12.____
     LNCR 5728
     WAEB 5368

13. NTWB 7948 13.____
     RABL 1385
     TAEF 9360

14. LWRB 5417 14.____
     RLWN 1647
     CBWA 2843

15. ABTC 3792 15.____
     WCER 5261
     AWCN 3417

16. Your job often brings you into contact with the public. Of the following, it would be *MOST* 16.____ desirable to explain the reasons for official actions to people coming into your office for assistance because such explanations

    A. help build greater understanding between the public and your agency
    B. help build greater self-confidence in city employees
    C. convince the public that nothing they do can upset a city employee
    D. show the public that city employees are intelligent

17. Assume that you strongly dislike one of your co-workers. 17.____
    You should *FIRST*

    A. discuss your feeling with the co-worker
    B. demand a transfer to another office
    C. suggest to your supervisor that the co-worker should be observed carefully
    D. try to figure out the reason for this dislike before you say or do anything

18. An office worker who has problems accepting authority is *MOST* likely to find it difficult to 18.____

    A. obey rules   B. understand people
    C. assist other employees   D. follow complex instructions

19. The employees in your office have taken a dislike to one person and frequently annoy 19.____ her. Your supervisor *should*

    A. transfer this person to another unit at the first opportunity
    B. try to find out the reason for the staff's attitude before doing anything about it
    C. threaten to transfer the first person observed bothering this person
    D. ignore the situation

20. Assume that your supervisor has asked a worker in your office to get a copy of a report 20.____ out of the files. You notice the worker has accidentally pulled out the wrong report.
    Of the following, the *BEST* way for you to handle this situation is to tell

    A. the worker about all the difficulties that will result from this error
    B. the worker about her mistake in a nice way
    C. the worker to ignore this error
    D. your supervisor that this worker needs more training in how to use the files

21. Filing systems differ in their efficiency. Which of the following is the *BEST* way to evaluate 21.____ the efficiency of a filing system?
    The

    A. number of times used per day
    B. amount of material that is received each day for filing
    C. amount of time it takes to locate material
    D. type of locking system used

22. In planning ahead so that a sufficient amount of general office supplies is always avail- 22.____ able, it would be *LEAST* important to find out the

    A. current office supply needs of the staff
    B. amount of office supplies used last year
    C. days and times that office supplies can be ordered
    D. agency goals and objectives

23. The *MAIN* reason for establishing routine office work procedures is that once a routine is established   23._____

    A. work need not be checked for accuracy
    B. all steps in the routine will take an equal amount of time to perform
    C. each time the job is repeated it will take less time to perform
    D. each step in the routine will not have to be planned all over again each time

24. When an office machine centrally located in an agency must be shut down for repairs, the bureaus and divisions using this machine should be informed of the   24._____

    A. expected length of time before the machine will be in operation again
    B. estimated cost of repairs
    C. efforts being made to avoid future repairs
    D. type of new equipment which the agency may buy in the future to replace the machine being repaired

25. If the day's work is properly scheduled, the *MOST* important result would be that the   25._____

    A. supervisor will not have to do much supervision
    B. employee will know what to do next
    C. employee will show greater initiative
    D. job will become routine

KEY (CORRECT ANSWERS)

1.	A		11.	C
2.	B		12.	B
3.	D		13.	D
4.	B		14.	B
5.	C		15.	A
6.	B		16.	A
7.	B		17.	D
8.	B		18.	A
9.	A		19.	B
10.	C		20.	B

21.	C
22.	D
23.	D
24.	A
25.	B

EXAMINATION SECTION
TEST 1

DIRECTIONS: Each question or incomplete statement is followed by several suggested answers or completions. Select the one that BEST answers the question or completes the statement. *PRINT THE LETTER OF THE CORRECT ANSWER IN THE SPACE AT THE RIGHT.*

1. Assume that a few co-workers meet near your desk and talk about personal matters during working hours. Lately, this practice has interfered with your work.
   In order to stop this practice, the BEST action for you to take FIRST is to

   A. ask your supervisor to put a stop to the co-workers' meeting near your desk
   B. discontinue any friendship with this group
   C. ask your co-workers not to meet near your desk
   D. request that your desk be moved to another location

1.____

2. In order to maintain office coverage during working hours, your supervisor has scheduled your lunch hour from 1 P.M. to 2 P.M. and your co-worker's lunch hour from 12 P.M. to 1 P.M. Lately, your co-worker has been returning late from lunch each day. As a result, you don't get a full hour since you must return to the office by 2 P.M.
   Of the following, the BEST action for you to take FIRST is to

   A. explain to your co-worker in a courteous manner that his lateness is interfering with your right to a full hour for lunch
   B. tell your co-worker that his lateness must stop or you will report him to your supervisor
   C. report your co-worker's lateness to your supervisor
   D. leave at 1 P.M. for lunch, whether your co-worker has returned or not

2.____

3. Assume that, as an office worker, one of your jobs is to open mail sent to your unit, read the mail for content, and send the mail to the appropriate person to handle. You accidentally open and begin to read a letter marked *personal* addressed to a co-worker.
   Of the following, the BEST action for you to take is to

   A. report to your supervisor that your co-worker is receiving personal mail at the office
   B. destroy the letter so that your co-worker does not know you saw it
   C. reseal the letter and place it on the co-worker's desk without saying anything
   D. bring the letter to your co-worker and explain that you opened it by accident

3.____

4. Suppose that in evaluating your work, your supervisor gives you an overall good rating, but states that you sometimes turn in work with careless errors.
   The BEST action for you to take would be to

   A. ask a co-worker who is good at details to proofread your work
   B. take time to do a careful job, paying more attention to detail
   C. continue working as usual since occasional errors are to be expected
   D. ask your supervisor if she would mind correcting your errors

4.____

5. Assume that you are taking a telephone message for a co-worker who is not in the office at the time.
   Of the following, the LEAST important item to write on the message is the

   A. length of the call   B. name of the caller
   C. time of the call   D. telephone number of the caller

5.____

Questions 6-13.

DIRECTIONS: Questions 6 through 13 each consist of a sentence which may or may not be an example of good English. The underlined parts of each sentence may be correct or incorrect. Examine each sentence, considering grammar, punctuation, spelling, and capitalization. If the English usage in the underlined parts of the sentence given is better than any of the changes in the underlined words suggested in Options B, C, or D, choose Option A. If the changes in the underlined words suggested in Options B, C, or D would make the sentence correct, choose the correct option. Do not choose an option that will change the meaning of the sentence.

6. This <u>Fall</u>, the office will be closed on <u>Columbus Day, October</u> 9th.   6._____

   A. Correct as is
   B. fall...Columbus Day, October
   C. Fall...columbus day, October
   D. fall...Columbus Day, october

7. This manual <u>discribes the duties performed</u> by an Office Aide.   7._____

   A. Correct as is
   B. describe the duties performed
   C. discribe the duties performed
   D. describes the duties performed

8. There <u>weren't no</u> paper in the supply closet.   8._____

   A. Correct as is   B. weren't any
   C. wasn't any   D. wasn't no

9. The new employees left <u>there</u> office to attend a meeting.   9._____

   A. Correct as is   B. they're
   C. their   D. thier

10. The office worker started working at <u>8;30 a.m.</u>   10._____

   A. Correct as is   B. 8:30 a.m.
   C. 8;30 a,m.   D. 8:30 am.

11. The <u>alphabet, or A to Z sequence</u> are the basis of most filing systems.   11._____

   A. Correct as is
   B. alphabet, or A to Z sequence, is
   C. alphabet, or A to Z sequence are
   D. alphabet, or A too Z sequence, is

12. <u>Those</u> file cabinets are five <u>feet</u> tall.   12._____

   A. Correct as is   B. Them...feet
   C. Those...foot   D. Them...foot

13. The Office Aide checked the <u>register and finding</u> the date of the meeting.   13._____

    A.   Correct as is   B.   regaster and finding
    C.   register and found   D.   regaster and found

Questions 14-21.

DIRECTIONS: Each of Questions 14 through 21 has two lists of numbers. Each list contains three sets of numbers. Check each of the three sets in the list on the right to see if they are the same as the corresponding set in the list on the left. Mark your answers:

    A.   If none of the sets in the right list are the same as those in the left list
    B.   if only one of the sets in the right list are the same as those in the left list
    C.   if only two of the sets in the right list are the same as those in the left list
    D.   if all three sets in the right list are the same as those in the left list

14.   7354183476   7354983476   14._____
       4474747744   4474747774
       57914302311   57914302311

15.   7143592185   7143892185   15._____
       8344517699   8344518699
       9178531263   9178531263

16.   2572114731   257214731   16._____
       8806835476   8806835476
       8255831246   8255831246

17.   331476853821   331476858621   17._____
       6976658532996   6976655832996
       3766042113715   3766042113745

18.   8806663315   8806663315   18._____
       74477138449   74477138449
       211756663666   211756663666

19.   990006966996   99000696996   19._____
       53022219743   53022219843
       4171171117717   4171171177717

20.   24400222433004   24400222433004   20._____
       5300030055000355   5300030055500355
       20000075532002022   20000075532002022

21.   611166640660001116   61116664066001116   21._____
       7111300117001100733   7111300117001100733
       26666446664476518   26666446664476518

Questions 22-25.

DIRECTIONS: Each of Questions 22 through 25 has two lists of names and addresses. Each list contains three sets of names and addresses. Check each of the three sets in the list on the right to see if they are the same as the corresponding set in the list on the left. Mark your answers:
- A. if none of the sets in the right list are the same as those in the left list
- B. if only one of the sets in the right list is the same as those in the left list
- C. if only two of the sets in the right list are the same as those in the left list
- D. if all three sets in the right list are the same as those in the left list

22. Mary T. Berlinger
2351 Hampton St.
Monsey, N.Y. 20117

Eduardo Benes
473 Kingston Avenue
Central Islip, N.Y. 11734

Alan Carrington Fuchs
17 Gnarled Hollow Road
Los Angeles, CA 91635

Mary T. Berlinger
2351 Hampton St.
Monsey, N.Y. 20117

Eduardo Benes
473 Kingston Avenue
Central Islip, N.Y. 11734

Alan Carrington Fuchs
17 Gnarled Hollow Road
Los Angeles, CA 91685

22._____

23. David John Jacobson
178 35 St. Apt. 4C
New York, N.Y. 00927

Ann-Marie Calonella
7243 South Ridge Blvd.
Bakersfield, CA 96714

Pauline M. Thompson
872 Linden Ave.
Houston, Texas 70321

David John Jacobson
178 53 St. Apt. 4C
New York, N.Y. 00927

Ann-Marie Calonella
7243 South Ridge Blvd.
Bakersfield, CA 96714

Pauline M. Thomson
872 Linden Ave.
Houston, Texas 70321

23._____

24. Chester LeRoy Masterton
152 Lacy Rd.
Kankakee, Ill. 54532

William Maloney
S. LaCrosse Pla.
Wausau, Wisconsin 52146

Cynthia V. Barnes
16 Pines Rd.
Greenpoint, Miss. 20376

Chester LeRoy Masterson
152 Lacy Rd.
Kankakee, Ill. 54532

William Maloney
S. LaCross Pla.
Wausau, Wisconsin 52146

Cynthia V. Barnes
16 Pines Rd.
Greenpoint, Miss. 20376

24._____

25. Marcel Jean Frontenac   Marcel Jean Frontenac   25.____
      6 Burton On The Water   6 Burton On The Water
      Calender, Me. 01471   Calender, Me. 01471

      J. Scott Marsden   J. Scott Marsden
      174 S. Tipton St.   174 Tipton St.
      Cleveland, Ohio   Cleveland, Ohio

      Lawrence T. Haney   Lawrence T. Haney
      171 McDonough St.   171 McDonough St.
      Decatur, Ga. 31304   Decatur, Ga. 31304

KEY (CORRECT ANSWERS)

1.	C		11.	B
2.	A		12.	A
3.	D		13.	C
4.	B		14.	B
5.	A		15.	B
6.	A		16.	C
7.	D		17.	A
8.	C		18.	D
9.	C		19.	A
10.	B		20.	C

21. C
22. C
23. B
24. B
25. C

TEST 2

DIRECTIONS: Each question or incomplete statement is followed by several suggested answers or completions. Select the one that BEST answers the question or completes the statement. *PRINT THE LETTER OF THE CORRECT ANSWER IN THE SPACE AT THE RIGHT.*

Questions 1-6.

DIRECTIONS: Questions 1 through 6 are to be answered SOLELY on the basis of the information contained in the following passage.

Duplicating is the process of making a number of identical copies of letters, documents, etc. from an original. Some duplicating processes make copies directly from the original document. Other duplicating processes require the preparation of a special master, and copies are then made from the master. Four of the most common duplicating processes are stencil, fluid, offset, and xerox.

In the stencil process, the typewriter is used to cut the words into a master called a stencil. Drawings, charts, or graphs can be cut into the stencil using a stylus. As many as 3,500 good-quality copies can be reproduced from one stencil. Various grades of finished paper from inexpensive mimeograph to expensive bond can be used.

The fluid process is a good method of copying from 50 to 125 good-quality copies from a master, which is prepared with a special dye. The master is placed on the duplicator, and special paper with a hard finish is moistened and then passed through the duplicator. Some of the dye on the master is dissolved, creating an impression on the paper. The impression becomes lighter as more copies are made; and once the dye on the master is used up, a new master must be made.

The offset process is the most adaptable office duplicating process because this process can be used for making a few copies or many copies. Masters can be made on paper or plastic for a few hundred copies, or on metal plates for as many as 75,000 copies. By using a special technique called photo-offset, charts, photographs, illustrations, or graphs can be reproduced on the master plate. The offset process is capable of producing large quantities of fine, top-quality copies on all types of finished paper.

The xerox process reproduces an exact duplicate from an original. It is the fastest duplicating method because the original material is placed directly on the duplicator, eliminating the need to make a special master. Any kind of paper can be used. The xerox process is the most expensive duplicating process; however, it is the best method of reproducing small quantities of good-quality copies of reports, letters, official documents, memos, or contracts.

1. Of the following, the MOST efficient method of reproducing 5,000 copies of a graph is   1._____

    A. stencil   B. fluid   C. offset   D. xerox

2. The offset process is the MOST adaptable office duplicating process because   2._____

    A. it is the quickest duplicating method
    B. it is the least expensive duplicating method
    C. it can produce a small number or large number of copies
    D. a softer master can be used over and over again

3. Which one of the following duplicating processes uses moistened paper?   3.____

   A. Stencil   B. Fluid   C. Offset   D. Xerox

4. The fluid process would be the BEST process to use for reproducing   4.____

   A. five copies of a school transcript
   B. fifty copies of a memo
   C. five hundred copies of a form letter
   D. five thousand copies of a chart

5. Which one of the following duplicating processes does NOT require a special master?   5.____

   A. Fluid   B. Xerox   C. Offset   D. Stencil

6. Xerox is NOT used for all duplicating jobs because   6.____

   A. it produces poor-quality copies
   B. the process is too expensive
   C. preparing the master is too time-consuming
   D. it cannot produce written reports

7. Assume a city agency has 775 office workers.   7.____
   If 2 out of 25 office workers were absent on a particular day, how many office workers
   reported to work on that day?

   A. 713   B. 744   C. 750   D. 773

Questions 8-11.

DIRECTIONS: In Questions 8 through 11, select the choice that is CLOSEST in meaning to
               the underlined word.

SAMPLE: This division reviews the fiscal reports of the agency.
               In this sentence, the word fiscal means MOST NEARLY
                    A. financial   B. critical   C. basic   D. personnel

               The correct answer is A, financial, because financial is closest to fiscal.

8. A central file eliminates the need to retain duplicate material.   8.____
   The word retain means MOST NEARLY

   A. keep   B. change   C. locate   D. process

9. Filing is a routine office task.   9.____
   Routine means MOST NEARLY

   A. proper   B. regular   C. simple   D. difficult

10. Sometimes a word, phrase, or sentence must be deleted to correct an error.   10.____
    Deleted means MOST NEARLY

    A. removed   B. added   C. expanded   D. improved

11. Your supervisor will <u>evaluate</u> your work.
    <u>Evaluate</u> means MOST NEARLY

    A. judge   B. list   C. assign   D. explain

11._____

Questions 12-19.

DIRECTIONS: The code table below shows 10 letters with matching numbers. For each Question 12 through 19, there are three sets of letters. Each set of letters is followed by a set of numbers which may or may not match their correct letter according to the code table. For each question, check all three sets of letters and numbers and mark your answer:
    A. if no pairs are correctly matched
    B. if only one pair is correctly matched
    C. if only two pairs are correctly matched
    D. if all three pairs are correctly matched

<u>CODE TABLE</u>

T	M	V	D	S	P	R	G	B	H
1	2	3	4	5	6	7	8	9	0

<u>Sample Question:</u>   TMVDSP - 123456
                       RGBHTM - 789011
                       DSPRGB - 256789

In the sample question above, the first set of numbers correctly matches its set of letters. But the second and third pairs contain mistakes. In the second pair, M is incorrectly matched with number 1. According to the code table, letter M should be correctly matched with number 2. In the third pair, the letter D is incorrectly matched with number 2. According to the code table, letter D should be correctly matched with number 4. Since only one of the pairs is correctly matched, the answer to this sample question is B.

12.   RSBMRM -   759262   12._____
       GDSRVH -   845730
       VDBRTM -   349713

13.   TGVSDR -   183247   13._____
       SMHRDP -   520647
       TRMHSR -   172057

14.   DSPRGM -   456782   14._____
       MVDBHT -   234902
       HPMDBT -   062491

15.   BVPTRD -   936184   15._____
       GDPHMB -   807029
       GMRHMV -   827032

16.   MGVRSH -   283750   16._____
       TRDMBS -   174295
       SPRMGV -   567283

17. SGBSDM - 489542   17.____
     MGHPTM - 290612
     MPBMHT - 269301

18. TDPBHM - 146902   18.____
     VPBMRS - 369275
     GDMBHM - 842902

19. MVPTBV - 236194   19.____
     PDRTMB - 647128
     BGTMSM - 981232

Questions 20-25.

DIRECTIONS: In each of Questions 20 through 25, the names of four people are given. For
              each question, choose as your answer the one of the four names given which
              should be filed FIRST according to the usual system of alphabetical filing of
              names, as described in the following paragraph.

    In filing names, you must start with the last name. Names are filed in order of the first let-
ter of the last name, then the second letter, etc. Therefore, BAILY would be filed before
BROWN, which would be filed before COLT. A name with fewer letters of the same type
comes first; i.e., Smith before Smithe. If the last names are the same, the names are filed
alphabetically by the first name. If the first name is an initial, a name with an initial would
come before a first name that starts with the same letter as the initial. Therefore, I. BROWN
would come before IRA BROWN. Finally, if both last name and first name are the same, the
name would be filed alphabetically by the middle name, one again an initial coming before a
middle name which starts with the same letter as the initial. If there is no middle name at all,
the name would come before those with middle initials or names.

Sample Question: A.   Lester Daniels
                   B.   William Dancer
                   C.   Nathan Danzig
                   D.   Dan Lester

The last names beginning with D are filed before the last name beginning with L. Since
DANIELS, DANCER, and DANZIG all begin with the same three letters, you must look at the
fourth letter of the last name to determine which name should be filed first. C comes before I or
Z in the alphabet, so DANCER is filed before DANIELS or DANZIG. Therefore, the answer to
the above sample question is B.

20.   A.   Scott Biala   B.   Mary Byala   20.____
      C.   Martin Baylor   D.   Francis Bauer

21.   A.   Howard J. Black   B.   Howard Black   21.____
      C.   J. Howard Black   D.   John H. Black

22.   A.   Theodora Garth Kingston B.   Theadore Barth Kingston   22.____
      C.   Thomas Kingston   D.   Thomas T. Kingston

23.   A.   Paulette Mary Huerta   B.   Paul M. Huerta   23.____
      C.   Paulette L. Huerta   D.   Peter A. Huerta

24. A. Martha Hunt Morgan   B. Martin Hunt Morgan   24.____
     C. Mary H. Morgan   D. Martine H. Morgan

25. A. James T. Meerschaum   B. James M. Mershum   25.____
     C. James F. Mearshaum   D. James N. Meshum

_____

KEY (CORRECT ANSWERS)

1.	C		11.	A
2.	C		12.	B
3.	B		13.	B
4.	B		14.	C
5.	B		15.	A
6.	B		16.	D
7.	A		17.	A
8.	A		18.	D
9.	B		19.	A
10.	A		20.	D

21. B
22. B
23. B
24. A
25. C

_____

TEST 3

DIRECTIONS: Each question or incomplete statement is followed by several suggested answers or completions. Select the one that BEST answers the question or completes the statement. *PRINT THE LETTER OF THE CORRECT ANSWER IN THE SPACE AT THE RIGHT.*

1. Which one of the following statements about proper telephone usage is NOT always correct?
   When answering the telephone, you should

   A. know whom you are speaking to
   B. give the caller your undivided attention
   C. identify yourself to the caller
   D. obtain the information the caller wishes before you do your other work

   1.____

2. Assume that, as a member of a worker's safety committee in your agency, you are responsible for encouraging other employees to follow correct safety practices. While you are working on your regular assignment, you observe an employee violating a safety rule.
   Of the following, the BEST action for you to take FIRST is to

   A. speak to the employee about safety practices and order him to stop violating the safety rule
   B. speak to the employee about safety practices and point out the safety rule he is violating
   C. bring the matter up in the next committee meeting
   D. report this violation of the safety rule to the employee's supervisor

   2.____

3. Assume that you have been temporarily assigned by your supervisor to do a job which you do not want to do. The BEST action for you to take is to

   A. discuss the job with your supervisor, explaining why you do not want to do it
   B. discuss the job with your supervisor and tell her that you will not do it
   C. ask a co-worker to take your place on this job
   D. do some other job that you like; your supervisor may give the job you do not like to someone else

   3.____

4. Assume that you keep the confidential personnel files of employees in your unit. A friend asks you to obtain some information from the file of one of your co-workers.
   The BEST action to take is to _____ to your friend.

   A. ask the co-worker if you can give the information
   B. ask your supervisor if you can give the information
   C. give the information
   D. refuse to give the information

   4.____

Questions 5-8.

DIRECTIONS: Questions 5 through 8 are to be answered SOLELY on the basis of the information contained in the following passage.

46

City government is committed to providing a safe and healthy work environment for all city employees. An effective agency safety program reduces accidents by educating employees about the types of careless acts which can cause accidents. Even in an office, accidents can happen. If each employee is aware of possible safety hazards, the number of accidents on the job can be reduced.

Careless use of office equipment can cause accidents and injuries. For example, file cabinet drawers which are filled with papers can be so heavy that the entire cabinet could tip over from the weight of one open drawer.

The bottom drawers of desks and file cabinets should never be left open since employees could easily trip over open drawers and injure themselves.

When reaching for objects on a high shelf, an employee should use a strong, sturdy object such as a step stool to stand on. Makeshift platforms made out of books, papers, or boxes can easily collapse. Even chairs can slide out from under foot, causing serious injury.

Even at an employee's desk, safety hazards can occur. Frayed or cut wires should be repaired or replaced immediately. Computers which are not firmly anchored to the desk or table could fall, causing injury.

Smoking is one of the major causes of fires in the office. A lighted match or improperly extinguished cigarette thrown into a wastebasket filled with paper could cause a major fire with possible loss of life. Where smoking is permitted, ashtrays should be used. Smoking is particularly dangerous in offices where flammable chemicals are used.

5. The goal of an effective safety program is to   5.____

   A. reduce office accidents
   B. stop employees from smoking on the job
   C. encourage employees to continue their education
   D. eliminate high shelves in offices

6. Desks and file cabinets can become safety hazards when   6.____

   A. their drawers are left open
   B. they are used as wastebaskets
   C. they are makeshift
   D. they are not anchored securely to the floor

7. Smoking is especially hazardous when it occurs   7.____

   A. near exposed wires
   B. in a crowded office
   C. in an area where flammable chemicals are used
   D. where books and papers are stored

8. Accidents are likely to occur when   8.____

   A. employees' desks are cluttered with books and papers
   B. employees are not aware of safety hazards
   C. employees close desk drawers
   D. step stools are used to reach high objects

9. Assume that part of your job as a worker in the accounting division of a city agency is to answer the telephone. When you first answer the telephone, it is LEAST important to tell the caller

    A. your title   B. your name
    C. the name of your unit   D. the name of your agency

9.____

10. Assume that you are assigned to work as a receptionist, and your duties are to answer phones, greet visitors, and do other general office work. You are busy with a routine job when several visitors approach your desk.
The BEST action to take is to

    A. ask the visitors to have a seat and assist them after your work is completed
    B. tell the visitors that you are busy and they should return at a more convenient time
    C. stop working long enough to assist the visitors
    D. continue working and wait for the visitors to ask you for assistance

10.____

11. Assume that your supervisor has chosen you to take a special course during working hours to learn a new payroll procedure. Although you know that you were chosen because of your good work record, a co-worker, who feels that he should have been chosen, has been telling everyone in your unit that the choice was unfair.
Of the following, the BEST way to handle this situation FIRST is to

    A. suggest to the co-worker that everything in life is unfair
    B. contact your union representative in case your co-worker presents a formal grievance
    C. tell your supervisor about your co-worker's complaints and let her handle the situation
    D. tell the co-worker that you were chosen because of your superior work record

11.____

12. Assume that while you are working on an assignment which must be completed quickly, a supervisor from another unit asks you to obtain information for her.
Of the following, the BEST way to respond to her request is to

    A. tell her to return in an hour since you are busy
    B. give her the names of some people in her own unit who could help her
    C. tell her you are busy and refer her to a co-worker
    D. tell her that you are busy and ask her if she could wait until you finish your assignment

12.____

13. A co-worker in your unit is often off from work because of illness. Your supervisor assigns the co-worker's work to you when she is not there. Lately, doing her work has interfered with your own job.
The BEST action for you to take FIRST is to

    A. discuss the problem with your supervisor
    B. complete your own work before starting your co-worker's work
    C. ask other workers in your unit to assist you
    D. work late in order to get the jobs done

13.____

14. During the month of June, 40,587 people attended a city-owned swimming pool. In July, 13,014 more people attended the swimming pool than the number that had attended in June. In August, 39,655 people attended the swimming pool.
The TOTAL number of people who attended the swimming pool during the months of June, July, and August was   14.____

   A. 80,242   B. 93,256   C. 133,843   D. 210,382

Questions 15-22.

DIRECTIONS: Questions 15 through 22 test how well you understand what you read. It will be necessary for you to read carefully because your answers to these questions must be based ONLY on the information in the following paragraphs.

The telephone directory is made up of two books. The first book consists of the introductory section and the alphabetical listing of names section. The second book is the classified directory (also known as the yellow pages). Many people who are familiar with one book do not realize how useful the other can be. The efficient office worker should become familiar with both books in order to make the best use of this important source of information.

The introductory section gives general instructions for finding numbers in the alphabetical listing and classified directory. This section also explains how to use the telephone company's many services, including the operator and information services, gives examples of charges for local and long-distance calls, and lists area codes for the entire country. In addition, this section provides a useful postal zip code map.

The alphabetical listing of names section lists the names, addresses, and telephone numbers of subscribers in an area. Guide names, or *telltales,* are on the top corner of each page. These guide names indicate the first and last name to be found on that page. *Telltales* help locate any particular name quickly. A cross-reference spelling is also given to help locate names which are spelled several different ways. City, state, and federal government agencies are listed under the major government heading. For example, an agency of the federal government would be listed under *United States Government.*

The classified directory, or yellow pages, is a separate book. In this section are advertising services, public transportation line maps, shopping guides, and listings of businesses arranged by the type of product or services they offer. This book is most useful when looking for the name or phone number of a business when all that is known is the type of product offered and the address, or when trying to locate a particular type of business in an area. Businesses listed in the classified directory can usually be found in the alphabetical listing of names section. When the name of the business is known, you will find the address or phone number more quickly in the alphabetical listing of names section.

15. The introductory section provides   15.____

    A. shopping guides   B. government listings
    C. business listings   D. information services

16. Advertising services would be found in the   16.____

    A. introductory section   B. alphabetical listing of names section
    C. classified directory   D. information services

17. According to the information in the above passage for locating government agencies, the
Information Office of the Department of Consumer Affairs of New York City government
would be alphabetically listed FIRST under

    A. *I* for Information Offices
    B. *D* for Department of Consumer Affairs
    C. *N* for New York City
    D. *G* for government

17.____

18. When the name of a business is known, the QUICKEST way to find the phone number is
to look in the

    A. classified directory
    B. introductory section
    C. alphabetical listing of names section
    D. advertising service section

18.____

19. The QUICKEST way to find the phone number of a business when the type of service a
business offers and its address is known is to look in the

    A. classified directory
    B. alphabetical listing of names section
    C. introductory section
    D. information service

19.____

20. What is a *telltale?*

    A. An alphabetical listing
    B. A guide name
    C. A map
    D. A cross-reference listing

20.____

21. The BEST way to find a postal zip code is to look in the

    A. classified directory
    B. introductory section
    C. alphabetical listing of names section
    D. government heading

21.____

22. To help find names which have several different spellings, the telephone directory provides

    A. cross-reference spelling   B. *telltales*
    C. spelling guides   D. advertising services

22.____

23. Assume that your agency has been given $2025 to purchase file cabinets.
If each file cabinet costs $135, how many file cabinets can your agency purchase?

    A. 8   B. 10   C. 15   D. 16

23.____

24. Assume that your unit ordered 14 staplers at a total cost of $30.20, and each stapler cost the same.
The cost of one stapler was MOST NEARLY

    A. $1.02   B. $1.61   C. $2.16   D. $2.26

24.____

25. Assume that you are responsible for counting and recording licensing fees collected by your department. On a particular day, your department collected in fees 40 checks in the amount of $6 each, 80 checks in the amount of $4 each, 45 twenty dollar bills, 30 ten dollar bills, 42 five dollar bills, and 186 one dollar bills.
The TOTAL amount in fees collected on that day was

    A. $1,406   B. $1,706   C. $2,156   D. $2,356

25.____

26. Assume that you are responsible for your agency's petty cash fund. During the month of February, you pay out 7 $2.00 subway fares and one taxi fare for $10.85. You pay out nothing else from the fund. At the end of February, you count the money left in the fund and find 3 one dollar bills, 4 quarters, 5 dimes, and 4 nickels. The amount of money you had available in the petty cash fund at the BEGINNING of February was

    A. $4.70   B. $16.35   C. $24.85   D. $29.55

26.____

27. You overhear your supervisor criticize a co-worker for handling equipment in an unsafe way. You feel that the criticism may be unfair.
Of the following, it would be BEST for you to

    A. take your co-worker aside and tell her how you feel about your supervisor's comments
    B. interrupt the discussion and defend your co-worker to your supervisor
    C. continue working as if you had not overheard the discussion
    D. make a list of other workers who have violated safety rules and give it to your supervisor

27.____

28. Assume that you have been assigned to work on a long-term project with an employee who is known for being uncooperative.
In beginning to work with this employee, it would be LEAST desirable for you to

    A. understand why the person is uncooperative
    B. act in a calm manner rather than an emotional manner
    C. be appreciative of the co-worker's work
    D. report the co-worker's lack of cooperation to your supervisor

28.____

29. Assume that you are assigned to sell tickets at a city-owned ice skating rink. An adult ticket costs $4.50, and a children's ticket costs $2.25. At the end of a day, you find that you have sold 36 adult tickets and 80 children's tickets.
The TOTAL amount of money you collected for that day was

    A. $244.80   B. $318.00   C. $342.00   D. $348.00

29.____

30. If each office worker files 487 index cards in one hour, how many cards can 26 office workers file in one hour?

    A. 10,662   B. 12,175   C. 12,662   D. 14,266

30.____

KEY (CORRECT ANSWERS)

1.	D		16.	C
2.	B		17.	C
3.	A		18.	C
4.	D		19.	A
5.	A		20.	B
6.	A		21.	B
7.	C		22.	A
8.	B		23.	C
9.	A		24.	C
10.	C		25.	C
11.	C		26.	D
12.	D		27.	C
13.	A		28.	D
14.	C		29.	C
15.	D		30.	C

EXAMINATION SECTION
TEST 1

DIRECTIONS: In each of the following groups of sentences, one of the four sentences contains one or more errors in grammar, sentence structure, English usage, spelling, diction, or punctuation. Select the INCORRECT sentence in each case.

1.   A.   It did not take him long to develop an interest in the great American pastime—baseball.
     B.   If you had made your way to the Whipsnade Zoo, you would have had an opportunity of seeing wild animals in more or less natural habitats.
     C.   How I should have liked to have spent a few more may in Paris!
     D.   Neither baseball pools nor any other form of gambling is allowed in or near the school.

1.____

2.   A.   If the bill were introduced, it would provoke endless debate.
     B.   Since George, with his two dogs, is to be with us, it might be better to rent a cabin.
     C.   He, not I, is the one to decide.
     D.   He is, however, one of those restless people who never seems content in his present environment.

2.____

3.   A.   Instead of looking disdainfully at London grime, think of it as a mantle of tradition.
     B.   Nobody but the pilot and the co-pilot was permitted to handle the mysterious package.
     C.   Not only is industry anxious to hire all available engineers, but they are being offered commissions by the armed forces.
     D.   For immediate service go direct to the store manager.

3.____

4.   A.   The delegates alighted and started off in a taxi, their baggage having been taken care of.
     B.   That kind of potatoes is grown in Idaho.
     C.   Besides Alan Stevens, there were eight officers of the organization on the dais.
     D.   As the delegates reached the convention hall late, they blamed their tardiness on the taxi driver.

4.____

5.   A.   The new system is superior from every point of view to the inefficient system in use until now.
     B.   The reason for the strike, you may recall, was because the union demanded a closed shop.
     C.   Who's to decide whether it is to be installed?
     D.   To suit Mr. Knolls, the new device will have to save time, money, and the dispositions of the employees.

5.____

6.   A.   Everyone can have a wonderful time in New York if they will just not try to see the entire city in one week.
     B.   Being a stranger in town myself, I know how you feel.
     C.   New York is a city of man-made wonders awe-inspiring as those found in nature.
     D.   He felt deep despair (as who has not?) at the evidence of man's inhumanity to man.

6.____

7.   A. In the recipe for custard, two cupfuls of milk will be enough.   7._____
       B. In the home economics classroom two tubs of clothes showed that it was not a day for cooking.
       C. It was 4:00 P.M. before the dishes were cleared away, washed, and put back into the closet.
       D. If only I had a fairy godmother like Cinderella!

8.   A. The zinnia has the more vivid color, but the violet is the sweeter-smelling.   8._____
       B. About three-fourths of the review I read was merely a summary of the story; the rest, criticism.
       C. I shall insist that he not be accepted as a member, since he is very bad-tempered.
       D. No sooner had he begun to speak when his auditors started to boo and hiss.

9.   A. Sandburg's autobiography, as well as his poems, are familiar to many readers.   9._____
       B. A series of authentic records of the American Indian tribes is being published.
       C. The Smokies are the home of the descendants of this brave tribe.
       D. Five dollars is really not too much to pay for a book of this type.

10. A. No one but her could have recognized him.   10._____
       B. She knew the stranger to be him whom she had given up as lost.
       C. He looked like he had been in some strange land where age advanced at a double pace.
       D. It is impossible to include that item; the agenda have already been mimeographed.

11. A. You have probably heard of the new innovation in the regular morning broadcast.   11._____
       B. During the broadcast you are expected to stand, to salute, and to sing the fourth stanza of "America."
       C. None of the rocks which form the solid crust of our planet is more than two billion years old.
       D. "I have finished my assignment," said the pupil. "May I go home now?"

12. A. The text makes the process of developing and sustaining a successful home zoo appear to be a pleasant and profitable one.   12._____
       B. The warmth and humor, the clear characterization of the Walmsey family, which includes three children, two dogs, and two cats, is such fun to read that this reviewer found herself reading it all over again.
       C. You will be glad, I am sure, to give the book to whoever among your young friends has displayed an interest in animals.
       D. The consensus among critics of children's literature is that the book is well worth the purchase price.

13. A. Participation in active sports produces both release from tension as well as physical well-being.   13._____
       B. The problem of taxes is still with them.
       C. Every boy and every girl in the auditorium was thrilled when the color guard appeared.
       D. At length our club decided to send two representatives to the meeting, you and me.

14. A. B. Nelson & Co. has a sale of dacron shirts today.   14.____
     B. Venetian blinds—called that although they probably did not originate in Venice—
       are no longer used as extensively as they were at one time.
     C. He determined to be guided by the opinion of whoever spoke first.
     D. There is often disagreement as to whom is the better Shakespearean actor,
       Evans or Gielgud.

15. A. Remains of an ancient civilization were found near Mexico City.   15.____
     B. It is interesting to compare the interior of one of the pyramids in Mexico to the
       interior of one of the pyramids in Egypt.
     C. In two days' journey you will be reminded of political upheavals comparable to
       the volcanic eruptions still visible and audible in parts of Mexico.
     D. There is little danger of the law's being broken, so drastic is the penalty.

16. A. The students in the dormitories were forbidden, unless they had special passes,   16.____
       from staying out after 11:00 P.M.
     B. The Student Court rendered a decision satisfactory to both the defendant and
       the accuser.
     C. Margarine is being substituted for butter to a considerable extent.
     D. In this school there are at least fifteen minor accidents a year which are due to
       this traffic violation.

17. A. Everyone at camp must have his medical certificate on file before participating in   17.____
       competitive sports.
     B. A crate of oranges were sent from Florida for all the children in Cabin Six.
     C. John and Danny's room looks as if they were prepared for inspection.
     D. Three miles is too far for a young child to walk.

18. A. Sailing along New England's craggy coastline, you will relive a bygone era of far-   18.____
       roving whalers and graceful clipper ships.
     B. The march of history is reenacted in folk festivals, outdoor pageants, and fiestas—
       local in theme, but national in import.
     C. Visiting the scenes of the past, our interest in American history is renewed and
       enlivened.
     D. What remained was a few unrecognizable fragments.

19. A. The game over, the spectators rushed out on the field and tore down the goal-   19.____
       posts.
     B. The situation was aggravated by disputes over the captaincy of the team.
     C. Yesterday they lay their uniforms aside with the usual end-of-the-season regret.
     D. It is sometimes thought that politics is not for the high-minded.

20. A. If I had built that house, I would have provided some sort of overhead protection   20.____
       from the drive to the front door.
     B. Our needs and hopes have been eloquently stated, but the initiative and follow-
       through has too often been left to others.
     C. I have tried this new method—in my fashion—and it worked very well.
     D. This is an essay in which the nature of intellectual curiosity and its relation to
       individual learning are analyzed.

21.   A. Since his pride was involved, Albert stated that he could not be expected to leave   21.____
           the question as to his loyalty go unanswered.
     B. General Sherman's interest in running for the highest office no longer remaining
           in doubt, the party leaders must look elsewhere for a candidate.
     C. Should you decide in the affirmative, I should be very pleased to give you the
           position.
     D. Although he had never known the applicant personally and although the man
           had been employed in the office for two years, the employment manager hesi-
           tated before making a decision.

22.   A. American politics demands that we stage an exciting game of "Musical Chairs"   22.____
           every four years.
     B. Pericles' decision to fight rallied the Athenians, including those who had formerly
           opposed him, to the common defense of the country.
     C. When you went into the dark office, whom were you looking for?
     D. In fact, Schultz also reportedly offered the officer a house for free in Westchester
           not to take him in as a racketeer.

23.   A. He was as old, if not older, than any other man in the entire community.   23.____
     B. Whomever the representative assembly chooses should be acceptable to the
           entire student body.
     C. One basis of the philosophy of the Existentialists is a concern for and an interest
           in the individual.
     D. If it had been necessary, the commissioner would have established regulations
           after conferences with the union representatives.

24.   A. The dog had lain in the car's shadow so long we had forgotten all about him.   24.____
     B. Is the fountain pen yours or theirs?
     C. Although we had less time to complete the test on Friday, we made fewer errors.
     D. "Whose coming in our car?" Mr. Porter asked.

25.   A. Every available member of the Sanitation Department work force, with the addition   25.
           of several thousand emergency workers, has been assigned to snow removal.
     B. Though almost overwhelmed by an unusual number of heavy snow storms, the
           commissioner's zeal never wavered.
     C. To remove the snow from the miles of city streets efficiently and swiftly requires
           manpower, equipment, and planning.
     D. Intelligence, devotion to duty, integrity—these are the commissioner's most signifi-
           cant qualities.

26.   A. With all that make-up on her face, she looked as though she were a clown.   26.____
     B. You will, I know, give the nomination for the scholarship to whoever among your
           students has achieved the highest average.
     C. Acting on my instructions, the custodian locked every door in the building.
     D. We were only halfway through the discussion when somebody voiced their opin-
           ion that long and dignified masculine tradition demanded concealing all the
           nobler sentiments.

27. A. A modern automobile should be kept in good working order so that its useful life may be lengthened.
     B. The control of traffic in the streets and on the highways of this city compares very favorably with any other city of similar size and wealth.
     C. When we invited you to the party, we hoped that you would come.
     D. Of the champion's three sons, none was more handsome or athletic than he.

27.____

28. A. All I wish to say, in conclusion, is that the rhetoricians spoken of attest the weakness of their rule by breaking it themselves.
     B. You will come and see us, won't you?
     C. The success of a small business enterprise depends on hard work, good location, and very frequently, factors beyond the full control of the business.
     D. Gracious means pleasing, attractive, a person who practices the amenities naturally and easily.

28.____

29. A. I prefer these kinds of books to those.
     B. Did he say, "The test will be on Saturday?"
     C. When we reviewed the report, we felt that we oughtn't to incur any further expenses.
     D. It's time to give the baby its bath.

29.____

30. A. None of the contestants, although they tried very hard, was able to answer the fourth question.
     B. Owing to the cooperation of all of the pupils, the Student Council membership drive was a great success.
     C. The one student candidate whom every member of the faculty agreed was the best qualified for the new position was almost overlooked in the election.
     D. Reptiles, amphibians, and predatory mammals swallow their prey whole or in large pieces, bones included.

30.____

KEY (CORRECT ANSWERS)

1.	C	11.	A	21.	A
2.	D	12.	B	22.	D
3.	C	13.	A	23.	A
4.	D	14.	D	24.	D
5.	B	15.	B	25.	B
6.	A	16.	A	26.	D
7.	D	17.	B	27.	B
8.	D	18.	C	28.	D
9.	A	19.	C	29.	A
10.	C	20.	B	30.	C

TEST 2

DIRECTIONS: In each of the following groups of sentences, one of the four sentences contains one or more errors in grammar, sentence structure, English usage, spelling, diction, or punctuation. Select the INCORRECT sentence in each case.

1. A. It is fatiguing to endure the guileless pantomine that dramatizes the theme, "The frivolous are blamable."
   B. I have always had a sincere interest and admiration for the important work of the teacher.
   C. He is one of the best pupils there are in our school.
   D. A predatory animal is voracious and rapacious.

   1._____

2. A. Baseball, football, and soccer have all been approved as extracurrircular activities. From either of them a coach can earn several hundreds of dollars each season.
   B. The search for truth is, and always has been, a subversive activity.
   C. Either competition for marks alone or memorized regurgitation of content smothers the spirit of inquiry.
   D. Actors who we know are second-rate are often starred in morning television programs.

   2._____

3. A. Do you believe that 15 bushels is enough of a load?
   B. At last it was Janet and Mary's turn to demonstrate their talents as dishwashers.
   C. How much happier my life could have been if I had had that kind of friends years ago!
   D. After I listened to the violinist and cellist, and enjoyed their interpretations, I hurried home to practice .

   3._____

4. A. In China today, there is insistence upon the doctor's giving greater attention to traditional medicine.
   B. No one in the audience dares refrain from hearty applause.
   C. The reason most educated Americans accept uncritically certain attitudes toward rising African nationalism is because they do not really know modern Africa.
   D. Lest the traveler concentrate too much on his stomach, the author has included notes on history.

   4._____

5. A. The farmer felt bad about his prize cow's being eliminated from competition.
   B. The teacher should make a distinction between the boy who occasionally misbehaves and he who is emotionally disturbed.
   C. These kinds of vegetables provide plenty of vitamins.
   D. Neither the soldiers in the field nor the captain in the barracks has any heart in the fight.

   5._____

6. A. "The ten or ten thousand commandments of languages are no longer graven on stone tablets," the English professor said.
   B. Ceramics, one of mankind's first arts, is having a renaissance after a century-long decline.
   C. White-maned and sturdy at 65, Mr. Fischer gave a program that few living pianists would either care or dare to present.
   D. The contrast between the virtuous countryside and the wicked city, long a part of American folklore, is something on which we can really collect very little data.

   6._____

7. A. Womens' clubs have been humorously but gently satirized by Helen Hokinson.
    B. Mr. Pollett asked, "Has everyone read Emily Dickinson's 'Chartless'?"
    C. In autumn the sugar maple is a golden yellow; the oak, a bronze and green; the huckleberry a fiery red.
    D. His seeming callousness was due to his almost morbid fear of appearing sentimental.

    7.____

8. A. Although I am willing to be lenient generally with children, I am determined that their parents shall pay reparations for this damage.
    B. Nearly one hundred dollars is the cost of the new, illustrated art book.
    C. The landings on the Normandy beaches in 1944 were in large part successful due to the supremacy of the Allied forces.
    D. Neither the mayor nor the members of the City Council want the city to secede from New York State.

    8.____

9. A. The "Matchbook Radio," weighing only nine ounces, is guaranteed to give better performance than any compact radio.
    B. The air-pump being broken, the vacuum was destroyed.
    C. One of the most remarkable phenomena of the bull market has been the rash of stock splits.
    D. In his frequent business ventures, Mr. Smith is the sort of man who often closes an important deal with a mere handshake.

    9.____

10. A. Gertrude Atherton writes to say that she thinks Frank Harris is a "spy and a rotter generally" whom she hopes will be shot.
    B. In ethical matters, one is reluctant to think of himself as merely a creature of habit.
    C. She writes so well that, were it not for the tyranny of space, there would be no end of quoting.
    D. An annoying accumulation of grammatical and syntactical misuses, that must be laid to the translator, mars the texture of otherwise well-ordered prose.

    10.____

11. A. Reston's deep, burning purpose is to influence favor-ably the course of important public events.
    B. Since it seemed so normal to them, neither Halifax nor Eden spoke much about his education.
    C. Not even his drink, carefully mixed in accordance with his instructions, tasted as well as usual.
    D. In his first gingerly experiment with popular elections, Pakistan's Ayub Khan got quite a surprise.

    11.____

12. A. In "The Pawnshop," Sydney Chaplin had brought in an alarm clock to pawn.
    B. The atmosphere is chill with winter's realism.
    C. Even the late Senator McCarthy handled the word "liberal" gingerly.
    D. Mrs. X and myself join with all the world in congratulating you on the birth of your royal son.

    12.____

13. A. Too slow a recognition can be disappointing, but too immediate a triumph can lead to a melancholy disillusion.
    B. If this man be Rajab Runjeet-Sing of Hindostan, thou hast done well in listening to his prayer.

    13.____

C. If we had made reservations for the 7 A.M. plane, we would not have been able to stay up late admiring the moon on the Ganges.

D. Ballantine's Ale is more than a thirst quencher; it's different than any other beer.

14. A. A change in programs was necessary and was effected in a very short time.   14.____

B. The teacher asked, "Has any of you failed to complete the homework assignment?"

C. Other minerals of this stage are dolomite, in small crystals, celestite, in slender prisma, and sylvanite, in prismatic crystals.

D. It is a national characteristic that is as true in peace as it is in war.

15. A. The idea of closed-circuit television is novel, instructive, and also serves as an   15.____
excellent device for teacher training.

B. The winner of the award was that attractive young woman, whom few people would have considered to be a serious contender.

C. The ladies' and children's clothing was strewn all around the room.

D. He was one of the marines who considered themselves brutally treated by the drill instructors.

16. A. The ambassador said, "I refer to all nations-all have the prime right to survive and   16.____
to take such steps as will best aid their survival."

B. England is one of Portugal's oldest allies, the two countries' association dating from the 12th century.

C. He is sensitive to sham and withdraws from people whom he feels are too free with compliments.

D. Do you know whether the data on the new refrigerators are statistically correct?

17. A. None are so deaf as those that will not hear.   17.____

B. If I had lent him that money, he would have gone free.

C. England's small expanse necessitates many people's living close together.

D. The hotel looked less dreary than the night before.

18. A. Either the mayor or the aldermen are to blame.   18.____

B. Unlike actual money, however, the value of trading stamps are only partly estimated on the basis of their buying power.

C. Approximately ten miles is the distance between my home and his.

D. One part of an animal which reveals his identity is his limbs.

19. A. That language is fluid, not static, is a commonplace; that words change their meanings, or have their meanings changed for them, is a familiar truth.   19.____

B. Steinberg's reading of Rimsky-Korsakov's Scheherazade is as wild, as pagan, and as Asiatic as his playing of Beethoven is noble.

C. The reason why they wanted to tour Europe was because they expected to find some bargains in native markets.

D. Although I realize that they are still legally children, I am determined that they shall be punished for their vandalism.

20. A. Of those who were graduated from high school, it appears that about 42 percent   20.____
actually went into farming.

B. Of all the people at the resort, she was the only one who looked good in sports clothes.

C. Mr. Carpenter feels that the opportunity to take part in the experiments, observations, and conclusions is making this year a most enjoyable one.
D. He not only wanted everyone to believe that he had found the missing link in man's ancestry but also to finance a further expedition into Africa.

21. A. If he had applied the brakes on time, all this confusion could have been avoided.   21.____
    B. Cities are man justifying himself to God.
    C. Like Caesar's wife, her private life was above suspicion.
    D. Politics makes strange bedfellows.

22. A. After three years his eyes had improved so much that he was able to resume the   22.____
    reading of law and to go on circuit.
    B. We watched the ballet dancers rehearse by standing at our window, which overlooked their outdoor stage.
    C. A great tongue of lava that had rolled down from one of the cones had piled up in the bed of the river and dispossessed the water of its course.
    D. There might come a time when there would be no living hand anywhere, no hand that could play music, and no music, not even, so long the reach of death, any remembered music.

23. A. Mama, brought up in the lively and prosperous world of Edinburgh professional   23.____
    and musical society, regarded marriage as the result of shaking up a number of young men and women at such festivities as dances, musical evenings, and picnics.
    B. Heroes of geology carried on the stirring search, sometimes painstakingly in their studies and sometimes dangerously at the edges of glaciers and volcanoes.
    C. What lies beneath the visible surface of the earth has always stirred the imagination of men.
    D. How could a man govern a nation when all he knew of the people whose affairs he would be trying to manage were the deputations that met him with band music and drums and pretty speeches?

24. A. Acting on His Majesty's orders, the Prime Minister's offices were invaded last night   24.____
    and ransacked.
    B. The answer, probably, is nothing.
    C. Since the agenda have been approved by the executive committee, I cannot approve your request to add a new item.
    D. Indeed, we now expect that science will on demand routinely produce miracle drugs.

25. A. Neither speech is to exceed fifteen minutes.   25.____
    B. A number of assemblages that are essentially alike, so much so that they were probably made by a single population, is called a culture.
    C. Like one man, for example, who sent in a portfolio of 31 different stocks worth less than $20,000 all told.
    D. I thought it all right to excuse them from class to watch the telecast of the presidential inauguration.

26. A. Why not join Gwen and myself at the concert?   26.____
     B. TV can be an invaluable aid to the teacher in presenting material clearly, effectively, and dramatically; however, it is not equally valuable in all steps of the learning process.
     C. I think we should treat them with a mixture of respect and irreverence: respect for their learning and experience, irreverence for any alleged infallibility.
     D. The apocryphal Acts of Paul is the work which contains a description of his appearance.

27. A. I said through tears that surprised me, "I would give this scholarship up, I would never touch the piano again, if only Papa would come back."   27.____
     B. The house was a 19th century copy of an Italian palace, with lawns, at that time yellow with daffodils, dropping to a canal.
     C. I think that he is as effective a broadcaster, if not more effective, than Ed Murrow.
     D. "He has always had such special difficulties. Oh, if I knew what to do!"

28. A. He knew the woman to be her whom he had dreamed about only the previous night.   28.____
     B. The creatures looked as though they had come from outer space, goggle-eyed, squat, and thin of limb.
     C. It is evident that they like nothing but dancing, racing around in hot-rod cars, and, hour after hour, to listen to the records of Elvis Presley.
     D. Twenty thousand dollars is really very little to pay for such a well-built house.

29. A. It was she, he knew!   29.____
     B. Could it have been he whom they called upon?
     C. Nobody but me knows what to do.
     D. In spite of frequent differences of opinion, he did not dislike his colleagues or they him.

30. A. The children's determination to find their dog almost resulted in tragedy.   30.____
     B. They spent the first night in a house that was unlocked and with no one at home.
     C. "What he asked me," said the boy, "was, 'Where can I find your father?'"
     D. It was the whimpering of a younger child and the comforting words of her brother that a member of the search-party heard about ten feet off the road.

KEY (CORRECT ANSWERS)

1.	B	11.	C	21.	C
2.	A	12.	D	22.	B
3.	D	13.	D	23.	D
4.	C	14.	C	24.	A
5.	B	15.	A	25.	C
6.	D	16.	C	26.	A
7.	A	17.	D	27.	C
8.	C	18.	B	28.	C
9.	A	19.	C	29.	D
10.	B	20.	D	30.	B

TEST 3

DIRECTIONS: In each of the following questions, there are four sentences, one of which contains an error in grammar, spelling, punctuation, usage, or diction. Choose the sentence which contains the error.

1. A. You have three books and she two, but hers costs more.   1.____
    B. Between you and me, the reason he is not going on a vacation is lack of money.
    C. He is my friend; nevertheless, I would not favor him in making my selection.
    D. The new battery of tests is designed to measure pupil achievement with greater
        accuracy.

2. A. The guidance counselor's job is to be of assistance to all of the students.   2.____
    B. The guidance counselors' job is to be of assistance to all of the students.
    C. The guidance counselors' job is to be of assistance to all of the students'.
    D. The guidance counselor's job is to be of assistance in the students' adjustment
        to school.

3. A. With your cooperation, I can achieve my goal.   3.____
    B. Giving me your help, I will be enabled to attain my objective.
    C. Given your able assistance, I can reach the goal we have agreed upon.
    D. Giving your assistance is most important if we are to meet with success.

4. A. You may have this book if you really want to read it.   4.____
    B. Although I have not sought it, this honor you have paid me is greatly appreciated.
    C. Truth, liberty, freedom, honor — what men have done in its name!
    D. It is futile to yearn for wealth when we know we cannot obtain it.

5. A. Be careful that you do not inadvertently pour the milk on the floor.   5.____
    B. The inference that you have drawn is utterly fallacious.
    C. I resent your implication of dishonesty; I am blameless
    D. Whether you bring the book to class or take it home, you are still responsible for
        the work.

6. A. Can you imagine me dancing, singing, clowning, and doing many other silly   6.____
        things?
    B. To lie, to falsify, and to commit perjury are tactics I must condemn.
    C. I spent the summer swimming, boating, fishing, and doing all else I could find at
        the lake.
    D. A student teacher is to observe, teach, and counsel — in short, she is to do all
        that a regular teacher does.

7. A. You will have gone by the time he arrives.   7.____
    B. Although I have attended college until recently, I left without getting my degree.
    C. I lived in Chicago for many years, but New York City has been my home for the
        past six months.
    D. I should not have gone before knowing what had to be done.

8. A. You must effect the changes whether you assent to them or not.   8.____
    B. Our personalities are complementary; that is the principal justification for our
        working together.

    C. Biographical information may be found in <u>Twentieth Century Authors, Currant Biography, Encyclopedia Britannica, and Who's Who.</u>

    D. The bridal party proceeded down the aisle to the altar in conformity with the hallowed rite.

9. A. I must admit that I haven't really given it much thought.   9.____

    B. Although you said you wanted the job completed speedily, I haven't barely begun it.

    C. It is hardly possible that such an incident could have actually occurred.

    D. It has been scarcely a week since I heard from you last.

10. A. You must not flaunt the parking regulations, no matter what you think of them.   10.____

    B. Regardless of public opinion, we will accept boys who are predelinquent though not incorrigible.

    C. An aggravation of the economic situation may lead to large-scale unemployment and widespread distress.

    D. Freedom of speech, press, and religion, along with positive measures to provide economic security, has been an attainable ideal in the western democracies.

11. A. It's a pity that the dog has hurt its paw.   11.____

    B. Enfeebled and emaciated, the old man passed away during the night.

    C. With baited breath, I huddled in a secluded corner of the garden.

    D. He is the aggrieved party in this internecine dispute.

12. A. Outflanked by the enemy fleet, ten of our ships were sunk, two were blown out of the water, and five were towed into port.   12.____

    B. He has torn himself away from human society, worn borrowed robes, and stole the possessions of others.

    C. Chosen for destruction and driven to the wall, I still shrank from a test of strength.

    D. Broken in mind and body, he swore he would rise once more to the challenge.

13. A. Who's to act as prosecutor if the evidence is lacking?   13.____

    B. That kind of book is flat, colorless, dull, and boring.

    C. Alice looks attractive in green, don't you think?

    D. We shall have a congenial group if we except only Phil.

14. A. Give the award to whomever, in your opinion, is most worthy.   14.____

    B. The gingko, according to the naturalists, should have gone with the pterodactyl and the brontosaurus, but it still survives.

    C. The toastmaster introduced the three guests: Paul Turnbull, prominent golfer; Eddy Fox, sports columnist; and Ben Doren, the team's manager.

    D. We should be happy to meet with you during the coming week.

15. A. Then Jim Hawkins began to listen in earnest and...but you know the rest of the story.   15.____

    B. At this very moment the group are disagreeing about the interpretation of the new law.

    C. New Yorkers speak somewhat differently from their neighbors across the Hudson.

    D. He would have been much happier if he would have followed his own precepts.

16. A. They oughtn't to consider themselves superior; they have little basis for such an opinion.   16.____
     B. Such consideration as you can give us will be appreciated.
     C. When Vin compared his own experiences with other men, he felt that he had not suffered unduly.
     D. Whatever he touched he embellished.

17. A. Of all our spring flowers, I think that hyacinths smell most sweet.   17.____
     B. Winter gardening under glass is fast regaining the popularity it had some thirty years ago.
     C. Microscopy is, with him, more than a fad; it is his raison d'etre.
     D. Here, Oswald, please bring this book to the English bookroom.

18. A. How many school boys have mouthed "to be or not to be" without having the slightest idea of the soliloquy's meaning!   18.____
     B. Phonetic spelling, with its upsetting of established conventions, has had rough going.
     C. The textbook can be an inspiration or a crutch; the best teachers and the poorest use them in different ways.
     D. He professed an abiding love for democracy, but his actions belied him.

19. A. Women's clothing has changed radically during the past few years; men's suits have scarcely changed at all.   19.____
     B. Turning on his heels as if to leave, his attention was suddenly distracted by the sound of a scuffle in the street.
     C. The boat had sunk at noon, but it was four p.m. before the first rescuers arrived on the spot.
     D. If Danny Kaye entertains, the meeting will be a success.

20. A. Thoreau maintained that the average man lives a life of quiet desperation.   20.____
     B. Journalese has unquestionably influenced Robertson's style—for the worse, alas!
     C. I wish that Jim might be here to listen to this stirring oration.
     D. Although the altitude of Mexico City is much higher, I found it less taxing than Acapulco.

21. A. All have applied, Daniel and she included.   21.____
     B. The jurors agreed that the accident had been clearly due to negligence and that a settlement should be made.
     C. At 10:15 a.m. promptly, the professor stalked majestically into the room, a book under his left arm.
     D. Please do not present your plan until thoroughly worked out in advance.

22. A. We should appreciate your prompt reply to our query.   22.____
     B. A principal should be democratic, sympathetic, and be able to take a firm position when necessary.
     C. He had four quests with him, Donald among the rest.
     D. That's the tiredest-looking puppy I've ever seen.

23. A. The treasurer and historian were absent from today's crucial session.   23.____
     B. He is a leading member of that group of English intellectuals which believes that society is growing increasingly blind, mad, and barbarous.

C. The book has lain untouched on the shelves for years.
D. By the time the news story is made public, he will, no doubt, already have been elected.

24. A. The secret is to be kept strictly between you and me.   24.____
    B. I planned to have gone to Canada during July and August.
    C. The group accepted Ted's suggestions with most of which we had all agreed.
    D. I objected strenuously (for who could be still?) to the plan proposed.

25. A. When these changes have been effected, I shall be in a better position to judge the   25.____
       merit of the suggestions.
    B. Whomever he selects will be our choice, too.
    C. He has not only taught in New York City, but in several western schools as well.
    D. Years before the first world war broke out, intelligent men had been forecasting the eruption.

26. A. It is surprising to discover that America now has less apple trees than it had fifty   26.____
       years ago.
    B. She smiled when called Betty, but she frowned upon those who dared call her Liz.
    C. He acted as though his suggestion could be the only one worth considering.
    D. Should he be selected, give him this note.

27. A. Jimmy and Joe were orphans whom our neighbors adopted when they were two   27.____
       years old.
    B. However he attempted to solve the cryptogram, the result was always the same- negative.
    C. The strikers have repeatedly shown that a number of them are in favor of their receiving retroactive pay.
    D. Those data have been verified by every statistician in the company.

28. A. The professor wanted to do advanced work in hydrodynamics, in which he had   28.____
       taken his Doctor of Philosophy degree.
    B. Eisenhower preferred to use the word "finalize" even though it was proscribed by precise grammarians.
    C. Would that I had been allowed to stay a minute longer!
    D. No sooner had the batter stepped into the box when a fastball came right at his head.

29. A. What look like two mechanical sentinels walk slowly back and forth before the gate.   29.____
    B. Apples were fewer this year; grapefruit, pulpier; and, of course, the amount of profit, smaller.
    C. If power were ever given to the incompetent, chaos would certainly result.
    D. Developed by the research engineers of Dupont, the government considers the new explosive a sure deterrent to war.

30. A. He gave two reasons: first, lack of funds; and second, he was disturbed by the   30.____
       thought of what his constituents would say.
    B. Although McIntyre had never tried his hand at fencing, he picked up the foils without a visible tremor.
    C. After the noise had died down, I found the visitor to be him.
    D. A number of the so-called guests had not actually been invited.

KEY (CORRECT ANSWERS)

1.	A	11.	C	21.	D
2.	C	12.	B	22.	B
3.	B	13.	B	23.	A
4.	C	14.	A	24.	B
5.	A	15.	D	25.	C
6.	A	16.	C	26.	A
7.	B	17.	D	27.	A
8.	C	18.	C	28.	D
9.	B	19.	B	29.	D
10.	A	20.	D	30.	A

———

TEST 4

DIRECTIONS: In each of the following groups of sentences, one of the four sentences contains one or more errors in grammar, sentence structure, diction, or punctuation. Select the INCORRECT sentence in each case.

1.   A.   There was absolutely no doubt in the minds of every member of her department against which of them the charges were being directed.
       B.   The former king of the cinema, now a radio actor, asserts that broadcasting is the ideal medium for the older actor who would like to retire, but who dreads complete leisure.
       C.   Oddly enough, when the average student has learned to love literature and to read rapidly for fun, he will derive incidentally most of the important values we are interested in.
       D.   He withheld the information from whoever asked for it.

      1.____

2.   A.   I met a painter whom critics think to be another Picasso.
       B.   The mother was apprehensive for the life of her cub.
       C.   Was it Brigham Young who declared, "This is the place?"
       D.   The owner, with all his assistants about him, was conspicuous at the game.

      2.____

3.   A.   Ham and eggs is a substantial Sunday supper.
       B.   He enjoyed playing chess in the evening, listening to the radio, and above all to read an hour or two before going to bed.
       C.   He asked, "Have you read 'Cimarron'?"
       D.   Despite her unusual complexion she looks good in somber colors.

      3.____

4.   A.   Boys of fourteen tend to enjoy stories of overt action tales of gore, hardship, the overcoming of fearful odds.
       B.   Our school has more students than any other in the borough.
       C.   By the time you receive this note I shall have left her home.
       D.   There is ample proof, in the reactions of our students to teacher quirks, that eccentricity is not necessarily a barrier to good teaching providing that the teacher is loved.

      4.____

5.   A.   Lew reported on the Tigers; Marvin, on the Cubs; and Kent, on the Braves.
       B.   Would that Pestalozzi were alive to see whither some of his ideas have led!
       C.   When one compares the Indians' record with the Braves, he is amazed at certain similarities.
       D.   Action, and not endless debates, is required at this stage.

      5.____

6.   A.   I rarely ever miss a picture produced by J. Arthur Rank.
       B.   Whose report is this? Elsa's?
       C.   After the detractors and the debunkers have had their say, America will still represent the most exciting ideal ever cherished; at least, no says Sandburg.
       D.   I regret to say that not one of the pupils in both honor classes did his unit conscientiously.

      6.____

7.   A.   The art of using cosmetics begins not with Madame Pompadour, not even with Cleopatra; the beginnings are lost in the mists of prehistory.
       B.   Were he completely intellectually honest, he'd be the first to admit his error.
       C.   Brock reported that Fred was at the meeting since nine o'clock.
       D.   The principal's policy was to assign the job to whoever, in either session, volunteered to do the work.

      7.____

8. A. I not only read the morning paper but many evening papers as well.   8._____
    B. Robert is not so tall as his brother.
    C. I could not but smile at the thought of his strange quandary.
    D. The gruesome experiences he'd had seemed to have had little effect upon his
       personality.

9. A. When the teacher returned to the room, he discovered that three of the culprits had   9._____
       slipped away.
    B. I cannot ever recall Bill going out of his way to be pleasant.
    C. Ability is only one of the qualities that are required for this position.
    D. The book had lain on the shelves for a year before Henry discovered it.

10. A. Men such as he are usually taken advantage of.   10._____
    B. Life is continually telling every one of us what his real weight is to the last grain of
       dust.
    C. I should have liked to go along with the rest, even though my foot still pained me
       from the skiing accident.
    D. Planning so carefully as he did for the future, all of us were surprised at the insig-
       nificance of his bequests.

11. A. His idiosyncrasies are mainly due to his unique upbringing.   11._____
    B. He inferred from her overwrought condition that she'd heard the bad news.
    C. Interpretations have been made that do not conflict with either religious teach-
       ings or scientific tenets.
    D. Neither the students nor the teacher were able to solve the problem.

12. A. He hoped that the members of the class did their home-work in preparation for the   12._____
       test.
    B. "Peace on earth"—how often through the centuries have men responded to the
       words' appeal!
    C. Even when a little girl, she would go to the library every Saturday.
    D. Had you made up your mind by three o'clock, you could have come with us.

13. A. No candidate having secured a majority on the first ballot, a second vote was   13._____
       taken.
    B. I have always considered Edna better than him.
    C. Being the county chess champion, he had to take on all comers.
    D. The equivocal prophecy foretold that Macbeth would not be as great, and yet
       much greater than Banquo.

14. A. Manslaughter is where a person is killed unlawfully but without premediation.   14._____
    B. In some cases neither of the candidates is able to show himself at his best.
    C. At the request of the defense attorney, the jury were polled and their individual
       verdicts recorded.
    D. The reason teenagers tend to follow the trend while openly declaring themselves
       non-conformists is that they are really insecure.

15. A. "Buxom" originally came from the Old English verb meaning "to bend."   15._____
    B. Whatever is in the oven smells delicious.
    C. Under such conditions one laments one's utter incapacity to be of any genuine
       service.
    D. The acrobat's widow eked out a miserable existence in dismal boarding houses
       and humble lodgings.

16.   A.   Owing to the ravages of the icy storm, communications within the area were practically obliterated.   16._____
      B.   Kwame Nkrumah, born in the primitive village of Nkroful in 1909, is pronounced as if it were spelled Qua-meh En-kroo-mah.
      C.   The wing of the plane collapsing under the impact, the fliers plunged to their death.
      D.   The detective, together with several of the uniformed men was decorated for outstanding bravery.

17.   A.   Mrs. Mary Johnson Aldrich, only daughter of the late Senator Aldrich, disclosed today plans for her third marriage, to Dr. H. Walter Sloan.   17._____
      B.   An excellent grade of synthetic rubber was discovered in 1954 by Goodrich-Gulf scientists.
      C.   It's now clear that the largest number of votes may go to the incumbent.
      D.   In the entire group, none was able to bear the heavy burden better than he.

18.   A.   The Wall St. operator worked strenuously until 3 o'clock and then took things easily for the rest of the day.   18._____
      B.   Many a challenge in the realm of politics is fraught with pitfalls for the unwary.
      C.   It was his intention to give due acknowledgement to whoever sent condolences.
      D.   Here is a statement that is unexceptionable: "America really did itself proud in the Tokyo Olympics."

19.   A.   Though he said they were all generous contributors, the tone in his voice implied they were not.   19._____
      B.   The sleeper could not have lain in bed much longer than he did.
      C.   It is generally held that English is one of the poorest taught subjects in high school today.
      D.   Take my book; if you use Bill's, you will find it's different from mine.

20.   A.   In today's market five dollars doesn't go very far.   20._____
      B.   Mary is just the kind of girl who everyone hopes will be the life of the party.
      C.   Ruthless, overbearing, and twisted mentally, the gangster proved a difficult witness before the committee.
      D.   The underdogs rallied bravely between every touchdown their burly opponents scored.

21.   A.   The rain having continued for a full hour with respite, the umpires called the game.   21._____
      B.   Who do you think will win the next presidential election?
      C.   The publisher offered no advance in royalties to the author nor a promise to advertise the book extensively.
      D.   The tally showed seventeen <u>ayes</u> for the resolution.

22.   A.   They thought they were cleverer than we.   22._____
      B.   If the United States would not have acted promptly, South Korea would have been lost in two weeks.
      C.   Everyone accepted the invitation except, oddly enough, him.
      D.   All that was left was a few blackened tree stumps.

23. A. "Have you ever," Bill asked smugly, "tried to change a flat tire before?"   23._____
     B. Because of the damp weather the window wouldn't rise.
     C. The delegates chosen to represent our association are you, he, and I.
     D. To me, at least, the remark clearly inferred that she disbelieved the story.

24. A. We tiptoed quietly into the room and—over went the lamp with a crash!   24._____
     B. The manager, together with his two coaches, were engaging the umpire in a bitter controversy.
     C. There seem to be many sources of friction between the sergeant and his men.
     D. Every one of the contestants was jumpy and excitable before the race.

25. A. Maxwell spoke as though he meant every word he said.   25._____
     B. Richness of color and diversity of design distinguishes the new collection of imported fabrics.
     C. Give the prize to whoever deserves it.
     D. You will find ladies' and girls' clothing on the fourth floor.

26. A. Are the family in agreement on vacation plans?   26._____
     B. It is one of those planes that fly faster than the speed of sound.
     C. "We drove through sixteen states on our latest jaunt," she declared, "we had only one detour."
     D. There were but three of us left after the first ballots had been tabulated.

27. A. Mr. Smith demurred at first, but they insisted on his accompanying them.   27._____
     B. The data are embodied in the majority report.
     C. Perry never has and never will accept that point of view.
     D. The courier brought encouraging news: negotiations were still in progress.

28. A. Though we had ridden nearly six hundred miles in one day, we felt relatively fresh and rested.   28._____
     B. Neither the two oaks nor the maple was affected by the gales of near-hurricane force.
     C. So that Carl would be at his best for the examination, his mother insisted he go to bed early the night before.
     D. The audience showed its approval vigorously; they applauded, stamped their feet, and whistled.

29. A. Ted would have liked to have solved the problem.   29._____
     B. Had you completed the job by the time you left?
     C. "Who does he think he is?" she indignantly demanded.
     D. They told us that they had gone on a cruise for their vacation, but we have heard none of the details of their trip.

30. A. "I myself," declared his sprightly dinner partner, "was once a ballerina."   30._____
     B. It seems to be I who am most concerned about the defeat
     C. Civilian defense is everybody's job, not just the worry of a few harried officials.
     D. The principal asked two of us, Carter and I, to assist in the gymnasium.

———

KEY (CORRECT ANSWERS)

1.	A	11.	D	21.	C
2.	C	12.	A	22.	B
3.	B	13.	D	23.	D
4.	D	14.	A	24.	B
5.	C	15.	D	25.	B
6.	A	16.	B	26.	C
7.	C	17.	B	27.	C
8.	A	18.	A	28.	D
9.	B	19.	C	29.	A
10.	D	20.	D	30.	D

SPELLING
EXAMINATION SECTION
TEST 1

DIRECTIONS: Each question or incomplete statement is followed by several suggested answers or completions. Select the one that BEST answers the question or completes the statement. *PRINT THE LETTER OF THE CORRECT ANSWER IN THE SPACE AT THE RIGHT.*

Questions 1-5.

DIRECTIONS: Questions 1 through 5 consist of four words. Indicate the letter of the word that is CORRECTLY spelled.

1. A. harassment   B. harrasment   1.____
    C. harasment   D. harrassment

2. A. maintainance   B. maintenence   2.____
    C. maintainence   D. maintenance

3. A. comparable   B. comprable   3.____
    C. comparible   D. commparable

4. A. suficient   B. sufficiant   4.____
    C. sufficient   D. suficiant

5. A. fairly   B. fairley   C. farely   D. fairlie   5.____

Questions 6-10.

DIRECTIONS: Questions 6 through 10 consist of four words. Indicate the letter of the word that is INCORRECTLY spelled.

6. A. pallor   B. ballid   C. ballet   D. pallid   6.____

7. A. urbane   B. surburbane
    C. interurban   D. urban

8. A. facial   B. physical   C. fiscle   D. muscle   8.____

9. A. interceed   B. benefited
    C. analogous   D. altogether

10. A. seizure   B. irrelevant
    C. inordinate   D. dissapproved

_____

KEY (CORRECT ANSWERS)

1. A   6. B
2. D   7. B
3. A   8. C
4. C   9. A
5. A   10. D

_____

TEST 2

DIRECTIONS: Each of Questions 1 through 15 consists of two words preceded by the letters A and B. In each question, one of the words may be spelled INCORRECTLY or both words may be spelled CORRECTLY. If one of the words in a question is spelled INCORRECTLY, print in the space at the right the capital letter preceding the INCORRECTLY spelled word. If both words are spelled CORRECTLY, print the letter C.

1.	A.	easely	B.	readily	1.___
2.	A.	pursue	B.	decend	2.___
3.	A.	measure	B.	laboratory	3.___
4.	A.	exausted	B.	traffic	4.___
5.	A.	discussion	B.	unpleasant	5.___
6.	A.	campaign	B.	murmer	6.___
7.	A.	guarantee	B.	sanatary	7.___
8.	A.	communication	B.	safty	8.___
9.	A.	numerus	B.	celebration	9.___
10.	A.	nourish	B.	begining	10.___
11.	A.	courious	B.	witness	11.___
12.	A.	undoubtedly	B.	thoroughly	12.___
13.	A.	accessible	B.	artifical	13.___
14.	A.	feild	B.	arranged	14.___
15.	A.	admittence	B.	hastily	15.___

KEY (CORRECT ANSWERS)

1.	A	6.	B	11.	A
2.	B	7.	B	12.	C
3.	C	8.	B	13.	B
4.	A	9.	A	14.	A
5.	C	10.	B	15.	A

TEST 3

DIRECTIONS: In each of the following sentences, one word is misspelled. Following each sentence is a list of four words taken from the sentence. Indicate the letter of the word which is MISSPELLED in the sentence. *PRINT THE LETTER OF THE CORRECT ANSWER IN THE SPACE AT THE RIGHT.*

1. The placing of any inflammable substance in any building, or the placing of any device or contrivence capable of producing fire, for the purpose of causing a fire is an attempt to burn.

    A. inflammable   B. substance
    C. device   D. contrivence

    1._____

2. The word *break* also means obtaining an entrance into a building by any artifice used for that purpose, or by colussion with any person therein.

    A. obtaining   B. entrance
    C. artifice   D. colussion

    2._____

3. Any person who with intent to provoke a breech of the peace causes a disturbance or is offensive to others may be deemed to have committed disorderly conduct.

    A. breech   B. disturbance
    C. offensive   D. committed

    3._____

4. When the offender inflicts a grevious harm upon the person from whose possession, or in whose presence, property is taken, he is guilty of robbery.

    A. offender   B. grevious
    C. possession   D. presence

    4._____

5. A person who wilfuly encourages or advises another person in attempting to take the latter's life is guilty of a felony.

    A. wilfuly   B. encourages
    C. advises   D. attempting

    5._____

6. He maliciously demurred to an ajournment of the proceedings.

    A. maliciously   B. demurred
    C. ajournment   D. proceedings

    6._____

7. His innocence at that time is irrelevant in view of his more recent villianous demeanor.

    A. innocence   B. irrelevant
    C. villianous   D. demeanor

    7._____

8. The mischievous boys aggrevated the annoyance of their neighbor.

    A. mischievous   B. aggrevated
    C. annoyance   D. neighbor

    8._____

9. While his perseverence was commendable, his judgment was debatable.

    A. perseverence   B. commendable
    C. judgment   D. debatable

    9._____

77

10. He was hoping the appeal would facilitate his aquittal.   10._____

    A. hoping   B. appeal
    C. facilitate   D. aquittal

11. It would be preferable for them to persue separate courses.   11._____

    A. preferable   B. persue
    C. separate   D. courses

12. The litigant was complimented on his persistance and achievement.   12._____

    A. litigant   B. complimented
    C. persistance   D. achievement

13. Ocassionally there are discrepancies in the descriptions of miscellaneous items.   13._____

    A. ocassionally   B. discrepancies
    C. descriptions   D. miscellaneous

14. The councilmanic seargent-at-arms enforced the prohibition.   14._____

    A. councilmanic   B. seargent-at-arms
    C. enforced   D. prohibition

15. The teacher had an ingenious device for maintaning attendance.   15._____

    A. ingenious   B. device
    C. maintaning   D. attendance

16. A worrysome situation has developed as a result of the assessment that absenteeism is increasing despite our conscientious efforts.   16._____

    A. worrysome   B. assessment
    C. absenteeism   D. conscientious

17. I concurred with the credit manager that it was practicable to charge purchases on a biennial basis, and the company agreed to adhear to this policy.   17._____

    A. concurred   B. practicable
    C. biennial   D. adhear

18. The pastor was chagrined and embarassed by the irreverent conduct of one of his parishioners.   18._____

    A. chagrined   B. embarassed
    C. irreverent   D. parishioners

19. His inate seriousness was belied by his flippant demeanor.   19._____

    A. inate   B. belied
    C. flippant   D. demeanor

20. It was exceedingly regrettable that the excessive number of challanges in the court delayed the start of the trial.   20._____

    A. exceedingly   B. regrettable
    C. excessive   D. challanges

KEY (CORRECT ANSWERS)

1.	D	11.	B
2.	D	12.	C
3.	A	13.	A
4.	B	14.	B
5.	A	15.	C
6.	C	16.	A
7.	C	17.	D
8.	B	18.	B
9.	A	19.	A
10.	D	20.	D

TEST 4

DIRECTIONS: Each question consists of three words. In each question, one of the words may be spelled incorrectly or all three may be spelled correctly. For each question. if one of the words is spelled INCORRECTLY, write the letter of the incorrect word in the space at the right. If all three words are spelled CORRECTLY, write the letter D in the space at the right.

SAMPLE I: (A) guide (B) department (C) stranger
SAMPLE II: (A) comply (B) valuable (C) window
In Sample I, departmint is incorrect. It should be spelled department. Therefore, B is the answer.
In Sample II, all three words are spelled correctly. Therefore, D is the answer.

1.	A. argument	B. reciept	C. complain	1.___
2.	A. sufficient	B. postpone	C. visible	2.___
3.	A. expirience	B. dissatisfy	C. alternate	3.___
4.	A. occurred	B. noticable	C. appendix	4.___
5.	A. anxious	B. guarantee	C. calender	5.___
6.	A. sincerely	B. affectionately	C. truly	6.___
7.	A. excellant	B. verify	C. important	7.___
8.	A. error	B. quality	C. enviroment	8.___
9.	A. exercise	B. advance	C. pressure	9.___
10.	A. citizen	B. expence	C. memory	10.___
11.	A. flexable	B. focus	C. forward	11.___

Questions 12-15.

DIRECTIONS: Each of Questions 12 through 15 consists of a group of four words. Examine each group carefully; then in the space at the right, indicate
A - if only one word in the group is spelled correctly
B - if two words in the group are spelled correctly
C - if three words in the group are spelled correctly
D - if all four words in the group are spelled correctly

12. Wendsday, particular, similar, hunderd   12.___

13. realize, judgment, opportunities, consistent   13.___

14. equel, principle, assistense, commitee   14.___

15. simultaneous, privilege, advise, ocassionaly   15.___

KEY (CORRECT ANSWERS)

1.	B	6.	D	11.	A
2.	D	7.	A	12.	B
3.	A	8.	C	13.	D
4.	B	9.	D	14.	A
5.	C	10.	B	15.	C

———

TEST 5

DIRECTIONS: Each of Questions 1 through 15 consists of two words preceded by the letters A and B. In each item, one of the words may be spelled INCORRECTLY or both words may be spelled CORRECTLY. If one of the words in a question is spelled INCORRECTLY, print in the space at the right the letter preceding the INCORRECTLY spelled word. If both words are spelled CORRECTLY, print the letter C.

1.	A.	justified	B.	offering	1._____
2.	A.	predjudice	B.	license	2._____
3.	A.	label	B.	pamphlet	3._____
4.	A.	bulletin	B.	physical	4._____
5.	A.	assure	B.	exceed	5._____
6.	A.	advantagous	B.	evident	6._____
7.	A.	benefit	B.	occured	7._____
8.	A.	acquire	B.	graditude	8._____
9.	A.	amenable	B.	boundry	9._____
10.	A.	deceive	B.	voluntary	10._____
11.	A.	imunity	B.	conciliate	11._____
12.	A.	acknoledge	B.	presume	12._____
13.	A.	substitute	B.	prespiration	13._____
14.	A.	reputible	B.	announce	14._____
15.	A.	luncheon	B.	wretched	15._____

KEY (CORRECT ANSWERS)

1. C	6. A	11. A
2. A	7. B	12. A
3. C	8. B	13. B
4. C	9. B	14. A
5. C	10. C	15. C

TEST 6

DIRECTIONS: Questions 1 through 15 contain lists of words, one of which is misspelled. Indicate the MISSPELLED word in each group. *PRINT THE LETTER OF THE CORRECT ANSWER IN THE SPACE AT THE RIGHT.*

1. A. felony   B. lacerate
    C. cancellation   D. seperate

2. A. batallion   B. beneficial
    C. miscellaneous   D. secretary

3. A. camouflage   B. changeable   C. embarass   D. inoculate   3.____

4. A. beneficial   B. disasterous
    C. incredible   D. miniature

5. A. auxilliary   B. hypocrisy   C. phlegm   D. vengeance   5.____

6. A. aisle   B. cemetary
    C. courtesy   D. extraordinary

7. A. crystallize   B. innoculate
    C. eminent   D. symmetrical

8. A. judgment   B. maintainance
    C. bouillon   D. eery

9. A. isosceles   B. ukulele   C. mayonaise   D. iridescent   9.____

10. A. remembrance   B. occurence
    C. correspondence   D. countenance

11. A. corpuscles   B. mischievous
    C. batchelor   D. bulletin

12. A. terrace   B. banister   C. concrete   D. masonery   12.____

13. A. balluster   B. gutter   C. latch   D. bridging   13.____

14. A. personnell   B. navel   C. therefor   D. emigrant   14.____

15. A. committee   B. submiting   15.____
    C. amendment   D. electorate

KEY (CORRECT ANSWERS)

1.	D	6.	B	11.	C
2.	A	7.	B	12.	D
3.	C	8.	B	13.	A
4.	B	9.	C	14.	A
5.	A	10.	B	15.	B

TEST 7

Questions 1-5.

DIRECTIONS: Questions 1 through 5 consist of groups of four words. Select answer:
A if only ONE word is spelled correctly in a group
B if TWO words are spelled correctly in a group
C if THREE words are spelled correctly in a group
D if all FOUR words are spelled correctly in a group

1. counterfeit, embarass, panicky, supercede   1.____

2. benefited, personnel, questionnaire, unparalelled   2.____

3. bankruptcy describable, proceed, vacuum   3.____

4. handicapped, mispell, offerred, pilgrimmage   4.____

5. corduroy, interfere, privilege, separator   5.____

Questions 6-10.

DIRECTIONS: Questions 6 through 10 consist of four pairs of words each. Some of the words are spelled correctly; others are spelled incorrectly. For each question, indicate in the space at the right the letter preceding that pair of words in which BOTH words are spelled CORRECTLY.

6. A. hygienic, inviegle   B. omniscience, pittance   6.____
    C. plagarize, nullify   D. seargent, perilous

7. A. auxilary, existence   B. pronounciation, accordance   7.____
    C. ignominy, indegence   D. suable, baccalaureate

8. A. discreet, inaudible   B. hypocrisy, currupt   8.____
    C. liquidate, maintainance   D. transparancy, onerous

9. A. facility, stimulent   B. frugel, sanitary   9.____
    C. monetary, prefatory   D. punctileous, credentials

10. A. bankruptsy, perceptible   B. disuade, resilient   10.____
    C. exhilerate, expectancy   D. panegyric, disparate

Questions 11-15

DIRECTIONS: Each question or incomplete statement is followed by several suggested answers or completions. Select the one that BEST answers the question or completes the statement. *PRINT THE LETTER OF THE CORRECT ANSWER IN THE SPACE AT THE RIGHT.*

11. The silent *e* must be retained when the suffix *-able* is added to the word   11.____

    A. argue   B. love   C. move   D. notice

12. The CORRECTLY spelled word in the choices below is   12.____

    A. kindergarden   B. zylophone
    C. hemorrhage   D. mayonaise

13. Of the following words, the one spelled CORRECTLY is   13.____

    A. begger   B. cemetary
    C. embarassed   D. coyote

14. Of the following words, the one spelled CORRECTLY is   14.____

    A. dandilion   B. wiry   C. sieze   D. rythmic

15. Of the following words, the one spelled CORRECTLY is   15.____

    A. beligerent   B. anihilation
    C. facetious   D. adversery

―――――

KEY (CORRECT ANSWERS)

1.	B	6.	B	11.	D
2.	C	7.	D	12.	C
3.	D	8.	A	13.	D
4.	A	9.	C	14.	B
5.	D	10.	D	15.	C

―――――

TEST 8

DIRECTIONS: In each of the following sentences, one word is misspelled. Following each sentence is a list of four words taken from the sentence. Indicate the letter of the word which is MISSPELLED. *PRINT THE LETTER OF THE CORRECT ANSWER IN THE SPACE AT THE RIGHT.*

1. If the administrator attempts to withold information, there is a good likelihood that there will be serious repercussions.

   A. administrator   B. withold
   C. likelihood   D. repercussions

1.____

2. He condescended to apologize, but we felt that a beligerent person should not occupy an influential position.

   A. condescended   B. apologize
   C. beligerent   D. influential

2.____

3. Despite the sporadic delinquent payments of his indebtedness, Mr. Johnson has been an exemplery customer.

   A. sporadic   B. delinquent
   C. indebtedness   D. exemplery

3.____

4. He was appreciative of the support he consistantly acquired, but he felt that he had waited an inordinate length of time for it.

   A. appreciative   B. consistantly
   C. acquired   D. inordinate

4.____

5. Undeniably they benefited from the establishment of a receivership, but the question of statutary limitations remained unresolved.

   A. undeniably   B. benefited
   C. receivership   D. statutary

5.____

6. Mr. Smith profered his hand as an indication that he considered it a viable contract, but Mr. Nelson alluded to the fact that his colleagues had not been consulted.

   A. profered   B. viable
   C. alluded   D. colleagues

6.____

7. The treatments were beneficial according to the optometrists, and the consensus was that minimal improvement could be expected.

   A. beneficial   B. optomotrists
   C. consensus   D. minimal

7.____

8. Her frivalous manner was unbecoming because the air of solemnity at the cemetery was pervasive.

   A. frivalous   B. solemnity
   C. cemetery   D. pervasive

8.____

9. The clandestine meetings were designed to make the two adversaries more amicable, but they served only to intensify their emnity.

   A. clandestine   B. adversaries
   C. amicable   D. emnity

9.____

10. Do you think that his innovative ideas and financial acumen will help stabalize the fluctu-
ations of the stock market?

    A. innovative   B. acumen
    C. stabalize   D. fluctuations

10._____

11. In order to keep a perpetual inventory, you will have to keep an uninterrupted surveil-
lance of all the miscellanious stock.

    A. perpetual   B. uninterrupted
    C. surveillance   D. miscellanious

11._____

12. She used the art of pursuasion on the children because she found that caustic remarks
had no perceptible effect on their behavior.

    A. pursuasion   B. caustic
    C. perceptible   D. effect

12._____

13. His sacreligious outbursts offended his constituents, and he was summarily removed
from office by the City Council.

    A. sacreligious   B. constituents
    C. summarily   D. Council

13._____

14. They exhorted the contestants to greater efforts, but the exhorbitant costs in terms of
energy expended resulted in a feeling of lethargy.

    A. exhorted   B. contestants
    C. exhorbitant   D. lethargy

14._____

15. Since he was knowledgable about illicit drugs, he was served with a subpoena to appear
for the prosecution.

    A. knowledgable   B. illicit
    C. subpoena   D. prosecution

15._____

16. In spite of his lucid statements, they denigrated his report and decided it should be suc-
cintly paraphrased.

    A. lucid   B. denigrated
    C. succintly   D. paraphrased

16._____

17. The discussion was not germane to the contraversy, but the indicted man's insistence on
further talk was allowed.

    A. germane   B. contraversy
    C. indicted   D. insistence

17._____

18. The legislators were enervated by the distances they had traveled during the election
year to fullfil their speaking engagements.

    A. legislators   B. enervated
    C. traveled   D. fullfil

18._____

19. The plaintiffs' attornies charged the defendant in the case with felonious assault.   19.____

    A. plaintiffs'   B. attornies
    C. defendant   D. felonious

20. It is symptomatic of the times that we try to placate all, but a proposal for new forms of   20.____
disciplinery action was promulgated by the staff.

    A. symptomatic   B. placate
    C. disciplinery   D. promulgated

KEY (CORRECT ANSWERS)

1.	B	6.	A	11.	D	16.	C
2.	C	7.	B	12.	A	17.	B
3.	D	8.	A	13.	A	18.	D
4.	B	9.	D	14.	C	19.	B
5.	D	10.	C	15.	A	20.	C

TEST 9

DIRECTIONS: Each of Questions 1 through 15 consists of a single word which is spelled either correctly or incorrectly. If the word is spelled CORRECTLY, you are to print the letter C (Correct) in the space at the right. If the word is spelled INCORRECTLY, you are to print the letter W (Wrong).

1. pospone   1.____

2. diffrent   2.____

3. height   3.____

4. carefully   4.____

5. ability   5.____

6. temper   6.____

7. deslike   7.____

8. seldem   8.____

9. alcohol   9.____

10. expense   10.____

11. vegatable   11.____

12. dispensary   12.____

13. specemin   13.____

14. allowance   14.____

15. exersise   15.____

KEY (CORRECT ANSWERS)

1.	W	6.	C	11.	W
2.	W	7.	W	12.	C
3.	C	8.	W	13.	W
4.	C	9.	C	14.	C
5.	C	10.	C	15.	W

TEST 10

DIRECTIONS: Each of Questions 1 through 10 consists of four words, one of which may be spelled incorrectly or all four words may be spelled correctly. If one of the words in a question is spelled incorrectly, print in the space at the right the capital letter preceding the word which is spelled INCORRECTLY. If all four words are spelled CORRECTLY, print the letter E.

1.	A.	dismissal	B.	collateral	C.	leisure	D.	proffession	1.___
2.	A.	subsidary	B.	outrageous	C.	liaison	D.	assessed	2.___
3.	A.	already	B.	changeable	C.	mischevous	D.	cylinder	3.___
4.	A.	supersede	B.	deceit	C.	dissension	D.	imminent	4.___
5.	A.	arguing	B.	contagious	C.	comparitive	D.	accessible	5.___
6.	A.	indelible	B.	existance	C.	presumptuous	D.	mileage	6.___
7.	A.	extention	B.	aggregate	C.	sustenance	D.	gratuitous	7.___
8.	A.	interrogate	B.	exaggeration	C.	vacillate	D.	moreover	8.___
9.	A.	parallel	B.	derogatory	C.	admissable	D.	appellate	9.___
10.	A.	safety	B.	cumalative	C.	disappear	D.	usable	10.___

KEY (CORRECT ANSWERS)

1.	D		6.	B
2.	A		7.	A
3.	C		8.	E
4.	E		9.	C
5.	C		10.	B

TEST 11

DIRECTIONS: Each of Questions 1 through 10 consists of four words, one of which may be spelled incorrectly or all four words may be spelled correctly. If one of the words in a question is spelled INCORRECTLY, print in the space at the right the capital letter preceding the word which is spelled incorrectly. If all four words are spelled CORRECTLY, print the letter E.

1. A. vehicular   B. gesticulate   1.____
    C. manageable   D. fullfil

2. A. inovation   B. onerous   2.____
    C. chastise   D. irresistible

3. A. familiarize   B. dissolution   3.____
    C. oscillate   D. superflous

4. A. census   B. defender   4.____
    C. adherence   D. inconceivable

5. A. voluminous   B. liberalize   5.____
    C. bankrupcy   D. conversion

6. A. justifiable   B. executor   6.____
    C. perpatrate   D. dispelled

7. A. boycott   B. abeyence   7.____
    C. enterprise   D. circular

8. A. spontaineous   B. dubious   8.____
    C. analyze   D. premonition

9. A. intelligible   B. apparently   9.____
    C. genuine   D. crucial

10. A. plentiful   B. ascertain   10.____
    C. carreer   D. preliminary

KEY (CORRECT ANSWERS)

1.	D	6.	C
2.	A	7.	B
3.	D	8.	A
4.	E	9.	E
5.	C	10.	C

TEST 12

DIRECTIONS: Questions 1 through 25 consist of four words each, of which one of the words may be spelled incorrectly or all four words may be spelled correctly. If one of the words in a question is spelled INCORRECTLY, print in the space at the right the capital letter preceding the word which is spelled incorrectly. If all four words are spelled CORRECTLY, print the letter E.

1. A. temporary   B. existance   1.___
    C. complimentary   D. altogether

2. A. privilege   B. changeable   2.___
    C. jeopardize   D. commitment

3. A. grievous   B. alloted   3.___
    C. outrageous   D. mortgage

4. A. tempermental   B. accommodating   4.___
    C. bookkeeping   D. panicky

5. A. auxiliary   B. indispensable   5.___
    C. ecstasy   D. fiery

6. A. dissappear   B. buoyant   6.___
    C. imminent   D. parallel

7. A. loosly   B. medicine   7.___
    C. schedule   D. defendant

8. A. endeavor   B. persuade   8.___
    C. retroactive   D. desparate

9. A. usage   B. servicable   9.___
    C. disadvantageous   D. remittance

10. A. beneficary   B. receipt   10.___
    C. excitable   D. implement

11. A. accompanying   B. intangible   11.___
    C. offerred   D. movable

12. A. controlling   B. seize   12.___
    C. repetitious   D. miscellaneous

13. A. installation   B. accommodation   13.___
    C. consistant   D. illuminate

14. A. incidentaly   B. privilege   14.___
    C. apparent   D. chargeable

15. A. prevalent   B. serial   15.___
    C. briefly   D. disatisfied

92

16.   A. reciprocal   B. concurrence   16.____
       C. persistence   D. withold

17.   A. deferred   B. suing   17.____
       C. fulfilled   D. pursuant

18.   A. questionnable   B. omission   18.____
       C. acknowledgment   D. insistent

19.   A. guarantee   B. committment   19.____
       C. mitigate   D. publicly

20.   A. prerogative   B. apprise   20.____
       C. extrordinary   D. continual

21.   A. arrogant   B. handicapped   21.____
       C. judicious   D. perennial

22.   A. permissable   B. deceive   22.____
       C. innumerable   D. retrieve

23.   A. notable   B. allegiance   23.____
       C. reimburse   D. illegal

24.   A. wholly   B. disbursement   24.____
       C. hindrance   D. conciliatory

25.   A. guidance   B. condemn   25.____
       C. publically   D. coercion

KEY (CORRECT ANSWERS)

1.	B		11.	C
2.	E		12.	E
3.	B		13.	C
4.	A		14.	A
5.	E		15.	D
6.	A		16.	D
7.	A		17.	E
8.	D		18.	A
9.	B		19.	B
10.	A		20.	C

21.	E
22.	A
23.	E
24.	E
25.	C

RECORD KEEPING
EXAMINATION SECTION
TEST 1

DIRECTIONS: Each question or incomplete statement is followed by several suggested answers or completions. Select the one that BEST answers the question or completes the statement. *PRINT THE LETTER OF THE CORRECT ANSWER IN THE SPACE AT THE RIGHT.*

Questions 1-15.

DIRECTIONS: Questions 1 through 15 are to be answered on the basis of the following list of company names below. Arrange a file alphabetically, word-by-word, disregarding punctuation, conjunctions, and apostrophes. Then answer the questions.

A Bee C Reading Materials
ABCO Parts
A Better Course for Test Preparation
AAA Auto Parts Co.
A-Z Auto Parts, Inc.
Aabar Books
Abbey, Joanne
Boman-Sylvan Law Firm
BMW Autowerks
C Q Service Company
Chappell-Murray, Inc.
E&E Life Insurance
Emcrisco
Gigi Arts
Gordon, Jon & Associates
SOS Plumbing
Schmidt, J.B. Co.

1. Which of these files should appear FIRST?   1.____

    A. ABCO Parts
    B. A Bee C Reading Materials
    C. A Better Course for Test Preparation
    D. AAA Auto Parts Co.

2. Which of these files should appear SECOND?   2.____

    A. A-Z Auto Parts, Inc.
    B. A Bee C Reading Materials
    C. A Better Course for Test Preparation
    D. AAA Auto Parts Co.

3. Which of these files should appear THIRD?   3.____

    A. ABCO Parts
    B. A Bee C Reading Materials
    C. Aabar Books
    D. AAA Auto Parts Co.

4. Which of these files should appear FOURTH?   4._____

   A. Aabar Books
   B. ABCO Parts
   C. Abbey, Joanne
   D. AAA Auto Parts Co.

5. Which of these files should appear LAST?   5._____

   A. Gordon, Jon & Associates
   B. Gigi Arts
   C. Schmidt, J.B. Co.
   D. SOS Plumbing

6. Which of these files should appear between A-Z Auto Parts, Inc. and Abbey, Joanne?   6._____

   A. A Bee C Reading Materials
   B. AAA Auto Parts Co.
   C. ABCO Parts
   D. A Better Course for Test Preparation

7. Which of these files should appear between ABCO Parts and Aabar Books?   7._____

   A. A Bee C Reading Materials
   B. Abbey, Joanne
   C. Aabar Books
   D. A-Z Auto Parts

8. Which of these files should appear between Abbey, Joanne and Boman-Sylvan Law Firm?   8._____

   A. A Better Course for Test Preparation
   B. BMW Autowerks
   C. Chappell-Murray, Inc.
   D. Aabar Books

9. Which of these files should appear between Abbey, Joanne and C Q Service?   9._____

   A. A-Z Auto Parts,Inc.   B. BMW Autowerks
   C. Choices A and B   D. Chappell-Murray, Inc.

10. Which of these files should appear between C Q Service Company and Emcrisco?   10._____

    A. Chappell-Murray, Inc.   B. E&E Life Insurance
    C. Gigi Arts   D. Choices A and B

11. Which of these files should NOT appear between C Q Service Company and E&E Life Insurance?   11._____

    A. Gordon, Jon & Associates
    B. Emcrisco
    C. Gigi Arts
    D. All of the above

12. Which of these files should appear between Chappell-Murray Inc., and Gigi Arts? 12.____

    A. CQ Service Inc. E&E Life Insurance, and Emcrisco
    B. Emcrisco, E&E Life Insurance, and Gordon, Jon & Associates
    C. E&E Life Insurance and Emcrisco
    D. Emcrisco and Gordon, Jon & Associates

13. Which of these files should appear between Gordon, Jon & Associates and SOS Plumbing? 13.____

    A. Gigi Arts
    B. Schmidt, J.B. Co.
    C. Choices A and B
    D. None of the above

14. Each of the choices lists the four files in their proper alphabetical order except 14.____

    A. E&E Life Insurance; Gigi Arts; Gordon, Jon & Associates; SOS Plumbing
    B. E&E Life Insurance; Emcrisco; Gigi Arts; SOS Plumbing
    C. Emcrisco; Gordon, Jon & Associates; SOS Plumbing; Schmidt, J.B. Co.
    D. Emcrisco; Gigi Arts; Gordon, Jon & Associates; SOS Plumbing

15. Which of the choices lists the four files in their proper alphabetical order? 15.____

    A. Gigi Arts; Gordon, Jon & Associates; SOS Plumbing; Schmidt, J.B. Co.
    B. Gordon, Jon & Associates; Gigi Arts; Schmidt, J.B. Co.; SOS Plumbing
    C. Gordon, Jon & Associates; Gigi Arts; SOS Plumbing; Schmidt, J.B. Co.
    D. Gigi Arts; Gordon, Jon & Associates; Schmidt, J.B. Co.; SOS Plumbing

16. The alphabetical filing order of two businesses with identical names is determined by the 16.____

    A. length of time each business has been operating
    B. addresses of the businesses
    C. last name of the company president
    D. none of the above

17. In an alphabetical filing system, if a business name includes a number, it should be 17.____

    A. disregarded
    B. considered a number and placed at the end of an alphabetical section
    C. treated as though it were written in words and alphabetized accordingly
    D. considered a number and placed at the beginning of an alphabetical section

18. If a business name includes a contraction (such as *don't* or *it's*), how should that word be treated in an alphabetical filing system? 18.____

    A. Divide the word into its separate parts and treat it as two words.
    B. Ignore the letters that come after the apostrophe.
    C. Ignore the word that contains the contraction.
    D. Ignore the apostrophe and consider all letters in the contraction.

19. In what order should the parts of an address be considered when using an alphabetical filing system? 19.____

    A. City or town; state; street name; house or building number
    B. State; city or town; street name; house or building number
    C. House or building number; street name; city or town; state
    D. Street name; city or town; state

20. A business record should be cross-referenced when a(n)   20.____

    A. organization is known by an abbreviated name
    B. business has a name change because of a sale, incorporation, or other reason
    C. business is known by a *coined* or common name which differs from a dictionary spelling
    D. all of the above

21. A geographical filing system is MOST effective when   21.____

    A. location is more important than name
    B. many names or titles sound alike
    C. dealing with companies who have offices all over the world
    D. filing personal and business files

Questions 22-25.

DIRECTIONS: Questions 22 through 25 are to be answered on the basis of the list of items below, which are to be filed geographically. Organize the items geographically and then answer the questions.

    1. University Press at Berkeley, U.S.
    2. Maria Sanchez, Mexico City, Mexico
    3. Great Expectations Ltd. in London, England
    4. Justice League, Cape Town, South Africa, Africa
    5. Crown Pearls Ltd. in London, England
    6. Joseph Prasad in London, England

22. Which of the following arrangements of the items is composed according to the policy of: 22.____
Continent, Country, City, Firm or Individual Name?

    A. 5, 3, 4, 6, 2, 1   B. 4, 5, 3, 6, 2, 1
    C. 1, 4, 5, 3, 6, 2   D. 4, 5, 3, 6, 1, 2

23. Which of the following files is arranged according to the policy of: *Continent, Country,*   23.____
City, Firm or Individual Name?

    A. South Africa. Africa. Cape Town. Justice League
    B. Mexico. Mexico City, Maria Sanchez
    C. North America. United States. Berkeley. University Press
    D. England. Europe. London. Prasad, Joseph

24. Which of the following arrangements of the items is composed according to the policy of: 24.____
Country, City, Firm or Individual Name?

    A. 5, 6, 3, 2, 4, 1   B. 1, 5, 6, 3, 2, 4
    C. 6, 5, 3, 2, 4, 1   D. 5, 3, 6, 2, 4, 1

25. Which of the following files is arranged according to a policy of: *Country, City, Firm or*   25.____
Individual Name?

    A. England. London. Crown Pearls Ltd.
    B. North America. United States. Berkeley. University Press
    C. Africa. Cape Town. Justice League
    D. Mexico City. Mexico. Maria Sanchez

26. Under which of the following circumstances would a phonetic filing system be MOST effective?   26.____

    A. When the person in charge of filing can't spell very well
    B. With large files with names that sound alike
    C. With large files with names that are spelled alike
    D. All of the above

Questions 27-29.

DIRECTIONS: Questions 27 through 29 are to be answered on the basis of the following list of numerical files.
    1. 391-023-100
    2. 361-132-170
    3. 385-732-200
    4. 381-432-150
    5. 391-632-387
    6. 361-423-303
    7. 391-123-271

27. Which of the following arrangements of the files follows a consecutive-digit system?   27.____

    A. 2, 3, 4, 1   B. 1, 5, 7, 3
    C. 2, 4, 3, 1   D. 3, 1, 5, 7

28. Which of the following arrangements follows a terminal-digit system?   28.____

    A. 1, 7, 2, 4, 3   B. 2, 1, 4, 5, 7
    C. 7, 6, 5, 4, 3   D. 1, 4, 2, 3, 7

29. Which of the following lists follows a middle-digit system?   29.____

    A. 1, 7, 2, 6, 4, 5, 3   B. 1, 2, 7, 4, 6, 5, 3
    C. 7, 2, 1, 3, 5, 6, 4   D. 7, 1, 2, 4, 6, 5, 3

Questions 30-31.

DIRECTIONS: Questions 30 and 31 are to be answered on the basis of the following information.
    1. Reconfirm Laura Bates appointment with James Caldecort on December 12 at 9:30 A.M.
    2. Laurence Kinder contact Julia Lucas on August 3 and set up a meeting for week of September 23 at 4 P.M.
    3. John Lutz contact Larry Waverly on August 3 and set up appointment for September 23 at 9:30 A.M.
    4. Call for tickets for Gerry Stanton August 21 for New Jersey on September 23, flight 143 at 4:43 P.M.

30. A chronological file for the above information would be

30.____

  A. 4, 3, 2, 1
  C. 4, 2, 3, 1

  B. 3, 2, 4, 1
  D. 3, 1, 2, 4

31. Using the above information, a chronological file for the date of September 23 would be

31.____

  A. 2, 3, 4   B. 3, 1, 4   C. 3, 2, 4   D. 4, 3, 2

Questions 32-34.

DIRECTIONS: Questions 32 through 34 are to be answered on the basis of the following information.
  1. Call Roger Epstein, Ashoke Naipaul, Jon Anderson, and Sarah Washington on April 19 at 1:00 P.M. to set up meeting with Alika D'Ornay for June 6 in New York.
  2. Call Martin Ames before noon on April 19 to confirm afternoon meeting with Bob Greenwood on April 20th
  3. Set up meeting room at noon for 2:30 P.M. meeting on April 19th;
  4. Ashley Stanton contact Bob Greenwood at 9:00 A.M. on April 20 and set up meeting for June 6 at 8:30 A.M.
  5. Carol Guiland contact Shelby Van Ness during afternoon of April 20 and set up meeting for June 6 at 10:00 A.M.
  6. Call airline and reserve tickets on June 6 for Roger Epstein trip *to* Denver on July 8
  7. Meeting at 2:30 P.M. on April 19th

32. A chronological file for all of the above information would be

32.____

  A. 2, 1, 3, 7, 5, 4, 6
  C. 3, 7, 1, 2, 5, 4, 6

  B. 3, 7, 2, 1, 4, 5, 6
  D. 2, 3, 1, 7, 4, 5, 6

33. A chronological file for the date of April 19th would be

33.____

  A. 2, 3, 7, 1
  C. 7, 1, 3, 2

  B. 2, 3, 1, 7
  D. 3, 7, 1, 2

34. Add the following information to the file, and then create a chronological file for April 20th:
  8. April 20: 3:00 P.M. meeting between Bob Greenwood and Martin Ames.

34.____

  A. 4, 5, 8   B. 4, 8, 5   C. 8, 5, 4   D. 5, 4, 8

35. The PRIMARY advantage of computer records filing over a manual system is

35.____

  A. speed of retrieval
  C. cost

  B. accuracy
  D. potential file loss

KEY (CORRECT ANSWERS)

1.	B		16.	B
2.	C		17.	C
3.	D		18.	D
4.	A		19.	A
5.	D		20.	D
6.	C		21.	A
7.	B		22.	B
8.	B		23.	C
9.	C		24.	D
10.	D		25.	A
11.	D		26.	B
12.	C		27.	C
13.	B		28.	D
14.	C		29.	A
15.	D		30.	B

31.	C
32.	D
33.	B
34.	A
35.	A

CLERICAL ABILITIES

EXAMINATION SECTION
TEST 1

DIRECTIONS: Each question or incomplete statement is followed by several suggested answers or completions. Select the one that BEST answers the question or completes the statement. *PRINT THE LETTER OF THE CORRECT ANSWER IN THE SPACE AT THE RIGHT.*

Questions 1-4.

DIRECTIONS: Questions 1 through 4 are to be answered on the basis of the information given below.

The most commonly used filing system and the one that is easiest to learn is alphabetical filing. This involves putting records in an A to Z order, according to the letters of the alphabet. The name of a person is filed by using the following order: first, the surname or last name; second, the first name; third, the middle name or middle initial. For example, *Henry C. Young* is filed under *Y* and thereafter under *Young, Henry C.* The name of a company is filed in the same way. For example, *Long Cabinet Co.* is filed under *L*, while *John T. Long Cabinet Co.* is filed under *L* and thereafter under *Long., John T. Cabinet Co.*

1. The one of the following which lists the names of persons in the CORRECT alphabetical order is:

    A. Mary Carrie, Helen Carrol, James Carson, John Carter
    B. James Carson, Mary Carrie, John Carter, Helen Carrol
    C. Helen Carrol, James Carson, John Carter, Mary Carrie
    D. John Carter, Helen Carrol, Mary Carrie, James Carson

1.____

2. The one of the following which lists the names of persons in the CORRECT alphabetical order is:

    A. Jones, John C.; Jones, John A.; Jones, John P.; Jones, John K.
    B. Jones, John P.; Jones, John K.; Jones, John C.; Jones, John A.
    C. Jones, John A.; Jones, John C.; Jones, John K.; Jones, John P.
    D. Jones, John K.; Jones, John C.; Jones, John A.; Jones, John P.

2.____

3. The one of the following which lists the names of the companies in the CORRECT alphabetical order is:

    A. Blane Co., Blake Co., Block Co., Blear Co.
    B. Blake Co., Blane Co., Blear Co., Block Co.
    C. Block Co., Blear Co., Blane Co., Blake Co.
    D. Blear Co., Blake Co., Blane Co., Block Co.

3.____

4. You are to return to the file an index card on *Barry C. Wayne Materials and Supplies Co.* Of the following, the CORRECT alphabetical group that you should return the index card to is

    A. A to G   B. H to M   C. N to S   D. T to Z

4.____

Questions 5-10.

DIRECTIONS: In each of Questions 5 through 10, the names of four people are given. For each question, choose as your answer the one of the four names given which should be filed FIRST according to the usual system of alphabetical filing of names, as described in the following paragraph.

In filing names, you must start with the last name. Names are filed in order of the first letter of the last name, then the second letter, etc. Therefore, BAILY would be filed before BROWN, which would be filed before COLT. A name with fewer letters of the same type comes first; i.e., Smith before Smithe. If the last names are the same, the names are filed alphabetically by the first name. If the first name is an initial, a name with an initial would come before a first name that starts with the same letter as the initial. Therefore, I. BROWN would come before IRA BROWN. Finally, if both last name and first name are the same, the name would be filed alphabetically by the middle name, once again an initial coming before a middle name which starts with the same letter as the initial. If there is no middle name at all, the name would come before those with middle initials or names.

Sample Question;   A.   Lester Daniels
                   B.   William Dancer
                   C.   Nathan Danzig
                   D.   Dan Lester

The last names beginning with D are filed before the last name beginning with L. Since DANIELS, DANCER, and DANZIG all begin with the same three letters, you must look at the fourth letter of the last name to determine which name should be filed first. C comes before I or Z in the alphabet, so DANCER is filed before DANIELS or DANZIG. Therefore, the answer to the above sample question is B.

5.   A.   Scott Biala   5.____
     B.   Mary Byala
     C.   Martin Baylor
     D.   Francis Bauer

6.   A.   Howard J. Black   6.____
     B.   Howard Black
     C.   J. Howard Black
     D.   John H. Black

7.   A.   Theodora Garth Kingston   7.____
     B.   Theadore Barth Kingston
     C.   Thomas Kingston
     D.   Thomas T. Kingston

8.   A.   Paulette Mary Huerta   8.____
     B.   Paul M. Huerta
     C.   Paulette L. Huerta
     D.   Peter A. Huerta

9. A. Martha Hunt Morgan
    B. Martin Hunt Morgan
    C. Mary H. Morgan
    D. Martine H. Morgan

9.____

10. A. James T. Meerschaum
    B. James M. Mershum
    C. James F. Mearshaum
    D. James N. Meshum

10.____

Questions 11-14.

DIRECTIONS: Questions 11 through 14 are to be answered SOLELY on the basis of the following information.

You are required to file various documents in file drawers which are labeled according to the following pattern:

DOCUMENTS

MEMOS		LETTERS	
File	Subject	File	Subject
84PM1 - (A-L)		84PC1 - (A-L)	
84PM2 - (M-Z)		84PC2 - (M-Z)	

REPORTS		INQUIRIES	
File	Subject	File	Subject
84PR1 - (A-L)		84PQ1 - (A-L)	
84PR2 - (M-Z)		84PQ2 - (M-Z)	

11. A letter dealing with a burglary should be filed in the drawer labeled

    A. 84PM1   B. 84PC1   C. 84PR1   D. 84PQ2

11.____

12. A report on Statistics should be found in the drawer labeled

    A. 84PM1   B. 84PC2   C. 84PR2   D. 84PQ2

12.____

13. An inquiry is received about parade permit procedures. It should be filed in the drawer labeled

    A. 84PM2   B. 84PC1   C. 84PR1   D. 84PQ2

13.____

14. A police officer has a question about a robbery report you filed.
    You should pull this file from the drawer labeled

    A. 84PM1   B. 84PM2   C. 84PR1   D. 84PR2

14.____

Questions 15-22.

DIRECTIONS: Each of Questions 15 through 22 consists of four or six numbered names. For each question, choose the option (A, B, C, or D) which indicates the order in which the names should be filed in accordance with the following filing instructions:
- File alphabetically according to last name, then first name, then middle initial.
- File according to each successive letter within a name.

- When comparing two names in which, the letters in the longer name are identical to the corresponding letters in the shorter name, the shorter name is filed first.
- When the last names are the same, initials are always filed before names beginning with the same letter.

15.   I.   Ralph Robinson   15._____
          II. Alfred Ross
          III. Luis Robles
          IV. James Roberts

The CORRECT filing sequence for the above names should be

    A. IV, II, I, III   B. I, IV, III, II
    C. III, IV, I, II   D. IV, I, III, II

16.   I.   Irwin Goodwin   16._____
          II. Inez Gonzalez
          III. Irene Goodman
          IV. Ira S. Goodwin
          V.   Ruth I. Goldstein
          VI. M.B. Goodman

The CORRECT filing sequence for the above names should be

    A. V, II, I, IV, III, VI   B. V, II, VI, III, IV, I
    C. V, II, III, VI, IV, I   D. V, II, III, VI, I, IV

17.   I.   George Allan   17._____
          II. Gregory Allen
          III. Gary Allen
          IV. George Allen

The CORRECT filing sequence for the above names should be

    A. IV, III, I, II   B. I, IV, II, III
    C. III, IV, I, II   D. I, III, IV, II

18.   I.   Simon Kauffman   18._____
          II. Leo Kaufman
          III. Robert Kaufmann
          IV. Paul Kauffmann

The CORRECT filing sequence for the above names should be

    A. I, IV, II, III   B. II, IV, III, I
    C. III, II, IV, I   D. I, II, III, IV

19.   I.   Roberta Williams   19._____
          II. Robin Wilson
          III. Roberta Wilson
          IV. Robin Williams

The CORRECT filing sequence for the above names should be

    A. III, II, IV, I   B. I, IV, III, II
    C. I, II, III, IV   D. III, I, II, IV

20.
    I. Lawrence Shultz
    II. Albert Schultz
    III. Theodore Schwartz
    IV. Thomas Schwarz
    V. Alvin Schultz
    VI. Leonard Shultz

20.____

The CORRECT filing sequence for the above names should be

  A. II, V, III, IV, I, VI   B. IV, III, V, I, II, VI
  C. II, V, I, VI, III, IV   D. I, VI, II, V, III, IV

21.
    I. McArdle
    II. Mayer
    III. Maletz
    IV. McNiff
    V. Meyer
    VI. MacMahon

21.____

The CORRECT filing sequence for the above names should be

  A. I, IV, VI, III, II, V   B. II, I, IV, VI, III, V
  C. VI, III, II, I, IV, V   D. VI, III, II, V, I, IV

22.
    I. Jack E. Johnson
    II. R.H. Jackson
    III. Bertha Jackson
    IV. J.T. Johnson
    V. Ann Johns
    VI. John Jacobs

22.____

The CORRECT filing sequence for the above names should be

  A. II, III, VI, V, IV, I   B. III, II, VI, V, IV, I
  C. VI, II, III, I, V, IV   D. III, II, VI, IV, V, I

Questions 23-30.

DIRECTIONS: The code table below shows 10 letters with matching numbers. For each question, there are three sets of letters. Each set of letters is followed by a set of numbers which may or may not match their correct letter according to the code table. For each question, check all three sets of letters and numbers and mark your answer:
    A. if no pairs are correctly matched
    B. if only one pair is correctly matched
    C. if only two pairs are correctly matched
    D. if all three pairs are correctly matched

<u>CODE TABLE</u>

T	M	V	D	S	P	R	G	B	H
1	2	3	4	5	6	7	8	9	0

<u>Sample Question:</u>   TMVDSP - 123456
                        RGBHTM - 789011
                        DSPRGB - 256789

In the sample question above, the first set of numbers correctly matches its set of letters. But the second and third pairs contain mistakes. In the second pair, M is incorrectly matched with number 1. According to the code table, letter M should be correctly matched with number 2. In the third pair, the letter D is incorrectly matched with number 2. According to the code table, letter D should be correctly matched with number 4. Since only one of the pairs is correctly matched, the answer to this sample question is B.

23. RSBMRM 759262
     GDSRVH 845730
     VDBRTM 349713

23.____

24. TGVSDR 183247
     SMHRDP 520647
     TRMHSR 172057

24.____

25. DSPRGM 456782
     MVDBHT 234902
     HPMDBT 062491

25.____

26. BVPTRD 936184
     GDPHMB 807029
     GMRHMV 827032

26.____

27. MGVRSH 283750
     TRDMBS 174295
     SPRMGV 567283

27.____

28. SGBSDM 489542
     MGHPTM 290612
     MPBMHT 269301

28.____

29. TDPBHM 146902
     VPBMRS 369275
     GDMBHM 842902

29.____

30. MVPTBV 236194
     PDRTMB 647128
     BGTMSM 981232

30.____

KEY (CORRECT ANSWERS)

1.	A	11.	B	21.	C
2.	C	12.	C	22.	B
3.	B	13.	D	23.	B
4.	D	14.	D	24.	B
5.	D	15.	D	25.	C
6.	B	16.	C	26.	A
7.	B	17.	D	27.	D
8.	B	18.	A	28.	A
9.	A	19.	B	29.	D
10.	C	20.	A	30.	A

TEST 2

DIRECTIONS: Each question or incomplete statement is followed by several suggested answers or completions. Select the one that BEST answers the question or completes the statement. *PRINT THE LETTER OF THE CORRECT ANSWER IN THE SPACE AT THE RIGHT.*

Questions 1-10.

DIRECTIONS: Questions 1 through 10 each consists of two columns, each containing four lines of names, numbers and/or addresses. For each question, compare the lines in Column I with the lines in Column II to see if they match exactly, and mark your answer A, B, C, or D, according to the following instructions:
- A. all four lines match exactly
- B. only three lines match exactly
- C. only two lines match exactly
- D. only one line matches exactly

	COLUMN I	COLUMN II	
1.	I. Earl Hodgson II. 1409870 III. Shore Ave. IV. Macon Rd.	Earl Hodgson 1408970 Schore Ave. Macon Rd.	1.____
2.	I. 9671485 II. 470 Astor Court III. Halprin, Phillip IV. Frank D. Poliseo	9671485 470 Astor Court Halperin, Phillip Frank D. Poliseo	2.____
3.	I. Tandem Associates II. 144-17 Northern Blvd. III. Alberta Forchi IV. Kings Park, NY 10751	Tandom Associates 144-17 Northern Blvd. Albert Forchi Kings Point, NY 10751	3.____
4.	I. Bertha C. McCormack II. Clayton, MO. III. 976-4242 IV. New City, NY 10951	Bertha C. McCormack Clayton, MO. 976-4242 New City, NY 10951	4.____
5.	I. George C. Morill II. Columbia, SC 29201 III. Louis Ingham IV. 3406 Forest Ave.	George C. Morrill Columbia, SD 29201 Louis Ingham 3406 Forest Ave.	5.____
6.	I. 506 S. Elliott Pl. II. Herbert Hall III. 4712 Rockaway Pkway IV. 169 E. 7 St.	506 S. Elliott Pl. Hurbert Hall 4712 Rockaway Pkway 169 E. 7 St.	6.____

		COLUMN I	COLUMN II	
7.	I.	345 Park Ave.	345 Park Pl.	7._____
	II.	Colman Oven Corp.	Coleman Oven Corp.	
	III.	Robert Conte	Robert Conti	
	IV.	6179846	6179846	
8.	I.	Grigori Schierber	Grigori Schierber	8._____
	II.	Des Moines, Iowa	Des Moines, Iowa	
	III.	Gouverneur Hospital	Gouverneur Hospital	
	IV.	91-35 Cresskill Pl.	91-35 Cresskill Pl.	
9.	I.	Jeffery Janssen	Jeffrey Janssen	9._____
	II.	8041071	8041071	
	III.	40 Rockefeller Plaza	40 Rockafeller Plaza	
	IV.	407 6 St.	406 7 St.	
10.	I.	5971996	5871996	10._____
	II.	3113 Knickerbocker Ave.	3113 Knickerbocker Ave.	
	III.	8434 Boston Post Rd.	8424 Boston Post Rd.	
	IV.	Penn Station	Penn Station	

Questions 11-14.

DIRECTIONS: Questions 11 through 14 are to be answered by looking at the four groups of names and addresses listed below (I, II, III, and IV) and then finding out the number of groups that have their corresponding numbered lines exactly the same.

GROUP I
Line 1. Richmond General Hospital
Line 2. Geriatric Clinic
Line 3. 3975 Paerdegat St.
Line 4 Loudonville, New York 11538

GROUP II
Richman General Hospital
Geriatric Clinic
3975 Peardegat St.
Londonville, New York 11538

GROUP III
Line 1. Richmond General Hospital
Line 2. Geriatric Clinic
Line 3. 3795 Paerdegat St.
Line 4. Loudonville, New York 11358

GROUP IV
Richmend General Hospital
Geriatric Clinic
3975 Paerdegat St.
Loudonville, New York 11538

11. In how many groups is line one exactly the same?   11._____

   A. Two   B. Three   C. Four   D. None

12. In how many groups is line two exactly the same?   12._____

   A. Two   B. Three   C. Four   D. None

13. In how many groups is line three exactly the same?   13._____

   A. Two   B. Three   C. Four   D. None

14. In how many groups is line four exactly the same?   14.____

   A. Two   B. Three   C. Four   D. None

Questions 15-18.

DIRECTIONS: Each of Questions 15 through 18 has two lists of names and addresses. Each
list contains three sets of names and addresses. Check each of the three sets
in the list on the right to see if they are the same as the corresponding set in
the list on the left. Mark your answers:
   A. if none of the sets in the right list are the same as those in the left list
   B. if only one of the sets in the right list is the same as those in the left
      list
   C. if only two of the sets in the right list are the same as those in the left
      list
   D. if all three sets in the right list are the same as those in the left list

15.   Mary T. Berlinger   Mary T. Berlinger   15.____
       2351 Hampton St.   2351 Hampton St.
       Monsey, N.Y. 20117   Monsey, N.Y. 20117

       Eduardo Benes   Eduardo Benes
       473 Kingston Avenue   473 Kingston Avenue
       Central Islip, N.Y. 11734   Central Islip, N.Y. 11734

       Alan Carrington Fuchs   Alan Carrington Fuchs
       17 Gnarled Hollow Road   17 Gnarled Hollow Road
       Los Angeles, CA 91635   Los Angeles, CA 91685

16.   David John Jacobson   David John Jacobson   16.____
       178 35 St. Apt. 4C   178 53 St. Apt. 4C
       New York, N.Y. 00927   New York, N.Y. 00927

       Ann-Marie Calonella   Ann-Marie Calonella
       7243 South Ridge Blvd.   7243 South Ridge Blvd.
       Bakersfield, CA 96714   Bakersfield, CA 96714

       Pauline M. Thompson   Pauline M. Thomson
       872 Linden Ave.   872 Linden Ave.
       Houston, Texas 70321   Houston, Texas 70321

17.   Chester LeRoy Masterton   Chester LeRoy Masterson   17.____
       152 Lacy Rd.   152 Lacy Rd.
       Kankakee, Ill. 54532   Kankakee, Ill. 54532

       William Maloney   William Maloney
       S. LaCrosse Pla.   S. LaCross Pla.
       Wausau, Wisconsin 52146   Wausau, Wisconsin 52146

       Cynthia V. Barnes   Cynthia V. Barnes
       16 Pines Rd.   16 Pines Rd.
       Greenpoint, Miss. 20376   Greenpoint, Miss. 20376

18.   Marcel Jean Frontenac   Marcel Jean Frontenac   18._____
        8 Burton On The Water   6 Burton On The Water
        Calender, Me. 01471   Calender, Me. 01471

        J. Scott Marsden   J. Scott Marsden
        174 S. Tipton St.   174 Tipton St.
        Cleveland, Ohio   Cleveland, Ohio

        Lawrence T. Haney   Lawrence T. Haney
        171 McDonough St.   171 McDonough St.
        Decatur, Ga. 31304   Decatur, Ga. 31304

Questions 19-26.

DIRECTIONS: Each of Questions 19 through 26 has two lists of numbers. Each list contains
              three sets of numbers. Check each of the three sets in the list on the right to
              see if they are the same as the corresponding set in the list on the left. Mark
              your answers:
              A.   if none of the sets in the right list are the same as those in the left list
              B.   if only one of the sets in the right list is the same as those in the left
                   list
              C.   if only two of the sets in the right list are the same as those in the left
                   list
              D.   if all three sets in the right list are the same as those in the left list

19.   7354183476   7354983476   19._____
      4474747744   4474747774
      57914302311   57914302311

20.   7143592185   7143892185   20._____
      8344517699   8344518699
      9178531263   9178531263

21.   2572114731   257214731   21._____
      8806835476   8806835476
      8255831246   8255831246

22.   331476853821   331476858621   22._____
      6976658532996   6976655832996
      3766042113715   3766042113745

23.   8806663315   8806663315   23._____
      74477138449   74477138449
      211756663666   211756663666

24.   990006966996   99000696996   24._____
      53022219743   53022219843
      4171171117717   4171171177717

25.   24400222433004   24400222433004   25._____
      5300030055000355   5300030055500355
      20000075532002022   20000075532002022

26. 611166640660001116   611166640660001116   26._____
     7111300117001100733   7111300117001100733
     26666446664476518   26666446664476518

Questions 27-30.

DIRECTIONS: Questions 27 through 30 are to be answered by picking the answer which is in the correct numerical order, from the lowest number to the highest number, in each question.

27.   A. 44533, 44518, 44516, 44547   27._____
     B. 44516, 44518, 44533, 44547
     C. 44547, 44533, 44518, 44516
     D. 44518, 44516, 44547, 44533

28.   A. 95587, 95593, 95601, 95620   28._____
     B. 95601, 95620, 95587, 95593
     C. 95593, 95587, 95601, 95620
     D. 95620, 95601, 95593, 95587

29.   A. 232212, 232208, 232232, 232223   29._____
     B. 232208, 232223, 232212, 232232
     C. 232208, 232212, 232223, 232232
     D. 232223, 232232, 232208, 232212

30.   A. 113419, 113521, 113462, 113588   30._____
     B. 113588, 113462, 113521, 113419
     C. 113521, 113588, 113419, 113462
     D. 113419, 113462, 113521, 113588

KEY (CORRECT ANSWERS)

1.	C	11.	A	21.	C
2.	B	12.	C	22.	A
3.	D	13.	A	23.	D
4.	A	14.	A	24.	A
5.	C	15.	C	25.	C
6.	B	16.	B	26.	C
7.	D	17.	B	27.	B
8.	A	18.	B	28.	A
9.	D	19.	B	29.	C
10.	C	20.	B	30.	D

FILING

EXAMINATION SECTION
TEST 1

DIRECTIONS: Each question from 1 through 10 contains four names. For each question, choose the name that should be *FIRST* if the four names were arranged in alphabetical order in accordance with the Rules for Alphabetical Filing given before. Read these rules carefully. Then, for each question, print in the space at the right the letter before the name that should be *FIRST* in alphabetical order.

SAMPLE QUESTION
A. Jane Earl   (2)
B. James A. Earle   (4)
C. James Earl   (1)
D. J. Earle   (3)

The numbers in parentheses show the proper alphabetical order in which these names should be filed. Since the name that should be filed *FIRST* is James Earl, the answer to the sample question is C.

1. A. Majorca Leather Goods   1._____
   B. Robert Maiorca and Sons
   C. Maintenance Management Corp.
   D. Majestic Carpet Mills

2. A. Municipal Telephone Service   2._____
   B. Municipal Reference Library
   C. Municipal Credit Union
   D. Municipal Broadcasting System

3. A. Robert B. Pierce   B. R. Bruce Pierce   3._____
   C. Ronald Pierce   D. Robert Bruce Pierce

4. A. Four Seasons Sports Club   4._____
   B. 14 Street Shopping Center
   C. Forty Thieves Restaurant
   D. 42nd St. Theaters

5. A. Franco Franceschini   B. Amos Franchini   5._____
   C. Sandra Franceschia   D. Lilie Franchinesca

6. A. Chas. A. Levine   B. Kurt Levene   6._____
   C. Charles Levine   D. Kurt E. Levene

7. A. Prof. Geo. Kinkaid   B. Mr. Alan Kinkaid   7._____
   C. Dr. Albert A. Kinkade   D. Kincade Liquors Inc.

8. A. Department of Public Events   8._____
    B. Office of the Public Administrator
    C. Queensborough Public Library
    D. Department of Public Health

9. A. Martin Luther King, Jr. Towers   9._____
    B. Metro North Plaza
    C. Manhattanville Houses
    D. Marble Hill Houses

10. A. Dr. Arthur Davids   10._____
    B. The David Check Cashing Service
    C. A. C. Davidsen
    D. Milton Davidoff

KEY (CORRECT ANSWERS)

1. C
2. D
3. B
4. D
5. C

6. B
7. D
8. B
9. A
10. B

TEST 2

DIRECTIONS: Each of questions 1 to 10 consists of four names. For each question, select the one of the four names that should be *THIRD* if the four names were arranged in alphabetical order in accordance with the Rules of Alphabetical Filing given before. Read these rules carefully. Then, for each question, print in the space at the right the letter preceding the name that should be *THIRD* in alphabetical order.

SAMPLE QUESTION

A. Fred Town   (2)
B. Jack Towne   (3)
C. D. Town   (1)
D. Jack S. Towne   (4)

The numbers in parentheses indicate the proper alphabetical order in which these names should be filed. Since the name that should be filed *THIRD* is Jack Towne, the answer is B.

1. A. Herbert Restman   B. H. Restman   1._____
    C. Harry Restmore   D. H. Restmore

2. A. Martha Eastwood   B. Martha E. Eastwood   2._____
    C. Martha Edna Eastwood   D. M. Eastwood

3. A. Timothy Macalan   B. Fred McAlden   3._____
    C. Thomas MacAllister   D. Mrs. Frank McAllen

4. A. Elm Trading Co.   4._____
    B. El Dorado Trucking Corp.
    C. James Eldred Jewelry Store
    D. Eldridge Printing, Inc.

5. A. Edward La Gabriel   B. Marie Doris Gabriel   5._____
    C. Marjorie N. Gabriel   D. Mrs. Marian Gabriel

6. A. Peter La Vance   B. George Van Meer   6._____
    C. Wallace De Vance   D. Leonard Vance

7. A. Fifth Avenue Book Shop   7._____
    B. Mr. Wm. A. Fifner
    C. 52nd Street Association
    D. Robert B. Fiffner

8. A. Dr. Chas. D. Peterson   B. Miss Irene F. Petersen   8._____
    C. Lawrence E. Peterson   D. Prof. N. A. Petersen

9. A. 71st Street Theater   B. The Seven Seas Corp.   9._____
    C. 7th Ave. Service Co.   D. Walter R. Sevan and Co.

10.   A.   Aerol Auto Body, Inc.
      B.   AAB Automotive Service Corp.
      C.   Acer Automotive
      D.   Alerte Automotive Corp.

10._____

––––––––

KEY (CORRECT ANSWERS)

1.   D
2.   B
3.   B
4.   D
5.   C

6.   D
7.   A
8.   A
9.   C
10. A

––––––––

TEST 3

DIRECTIONS: Same as for Test 2.

1. A. William Carver   B. Howard Cambell   1.____
    C. Arthur Chambers   D. Charles Banner

2. A. Paul Moore   B. William Moore   2.____
    C. Paul A. Moore   D. William Allen Moore

3. A. George Peters   B. Eric Petersen   3.____
    C. G. Peters   D. E. Petersen

4. A. Edward Hallam   B. Jos. Frank Hamilton   4.____
    C. Edward A. Hallam   D. Joseph F. Hamilton

5. A. Theodore Madison   B. Timothy McGill   5.____
    C. Thomas MacLane   D. Thomas A. Madison

6. A. William O'Hara   B. Arthur Gordon   6.____
    C. James DeGraff   D. Anne von Glatin

7. A. Charles Green   B. Chas. T. Greene   7.____
    C. Charles Thomas Greene   D. Wm. A. Greene

8. A. John Foss Insurance Co. B. New World Stove Co.   8.____
    C. 14th Street Dress Shop D. Arthur Stein Paper Co.

9. A. Gold Trucking Co.   B. B. 8th Ave. Garage   9.____
    C. The First National Bank D. The Century Novelty Co.

10. A. F. L. Doskow   B. Natalie S. Doskow   10.____
    C. Samuel B. Doskow   D. Arthur G. Doskor

KEY (CORRECT ANSWERS)

1. A
2. B
3. D
4. D
5. D

6. A
7. C
8. B
9. C
10. B

TEST 4

DIRECTIONS: Each question from 1 through 10 consists of four names. For each question, choose the one of the four names that should be *LAST* if the four names were arranged in alphabetical order in accordance with the Rules for Alphabetical Filing given before. Read these rules carefully. Then, for each question, print in the space at the right the letter before the name that should be *LAST* in alphabetical order.

SAMPLE QUESTION

A. Jane Earl (2)
B. James A. Earle (4)
C. James Earl (1)
D. J. Earle (3)

The numbers in parentheses show the proper alphabetical order in which these names should be filed. Since the name that should be filed *LAST* is James A. Earle, the answer to the sample question is B.

1. A. Corral, Dr. Robert   B. Carrale, Prof. Robert   1.____
    C. Corren, R.   D. Corret, Ron

2. A. Rivera, Ilena   B. Riviera, Ilene   2.____
    C. Rivere, I.   D. Riviera Ice-Cream Co.

3. A. VonHogel, George   B. Volper, Gary   3.____
    C. Vonner, G.   D. Van Pefel, Gregory

4. A. David Kallish Stationery Co.   4.____
    B. Emerson Microfilm Company
    C. David Kalder Industrial Engineers Associated
    D. 5th Avenue Office Furniture Co.

5. A. A. Bennet, C.   B. Benett, Chuck   5.____
    C. Bennet, Chas.   D. Bennett, Charles

6. A. The Board of Higher Education   6.____
    B. National Education Commission
    C. Eakin, Hugh
    D. Nathan, Ellen

7. A. McCloud, I.   B. MacGowen, Ian   7.____
    C. McGowen, Arthur   D. Macale, Sean

8. A. Devine, Sarah   B. Devine, S.   8.____
    C. Devine, Sara H.   D. Devin, Sarah

9. A. Milstein, Louis   B. Milrad, Abraham P.   9.____
    C. Milstein, Herman   D. Milstien, Harold G.

10. A. Herfield, Lester L.   B. Herbstman, Nathan   10.____
    C. Henricksen, Ole A.   D. Herfeld, Burton G.

KEY (CORRECT ANSWERS)

1. D
2. B
3. C
4. A
5. D

6. B
7. C
8. A
9. D
10. A

———

TEST 5

DIRECTIONS: Same as for Test 4.

1. A. Francis Lattimore   B. H. Latham   1.____
    C. G. Lattimore   D. Hugh Latham

2. A. Thomas B. Morgan   B. B. Thomas Morgan   2.____
    C. T. Morgan   D. Thomas Bertram Morgan

3. A. Lawrence A. Villon   B. Chas. Valente   3.____
    C. Charles M. Valent   D. Lawrence De Villon

4. A. Alfred Devance   B. A. R. D'Amico   4.____
    C. Arnold De Vincent   D. A. De Pino

5. A. Dr. Milton A. Bergmann   B. Miss Evelyn M. Bergmenn   5.____
    C. Prof. E. N. Bergmenn   D. Mrs. L. B. Bergmann

6. A. George MacDougald   B. Thomas McHern   6.____
    C. William Macholt   D. Frank McHenry

7. A. Third National Bank   B. Robt. Tempkin Corp.   7.____
    C. 32nd Street Carpet Co.   D. Wm. Templeton, Inc.

8. A. Mary Lobell Art Shop   B. John La Marca, Inc   8.____
    C. Lawyers' Guild   D. Frank Le Goff Studios

9. A. 9th Avenue Garage   B. Jos. Nuren Food Co.   9.____
    C. The New Book Store   D. Novelty Card Corp.

10. A. Murphy's Moving & Storage, Inc.   10.____
     B. Mid-Island Van Lines Corporation
     C. Mollone Bros. Moving & Storage, Inc.
     D. McShane Moving & Storage, Inc.

KEY (CORRECT ANSWERS)

1. C
2. D
3. A
4. C
5. B

6. B
7. C
8. A
9. B
10. A

TEST 6

DIRECTIONS: Each question contains four names numbered from 1 through 4 but not necessarily numbered in correct filing order. Answer each question by choosing the letter corresponding to the *CORRECT* filing order of the four names in accordance with the Rules for Alphabetic Filing given before. *PRINT THE LETTER OF THE CORRECT ANSWER IN THE SPACE AT THE RIGHT.*

SAMPLE QUESTION

1. Robert J. Smith
2. R. Jeffrey Smith
3. Dr. A. Smythe
4. Allen R. Smithers

A. 1, 2, 3, 4   B. 3, 1, 2, 4   C. 2, 1, 4, 3   D. 3, 2, 1, 4

Since the correct filing order, in accordance with the above rules, is 2, 1, 4, 3, the correct answer is C.

1.
   1. J. Chester VanClief
   2. John C. VanClief
   3. J. VanCleve
   4. Mary L. Vance

   A. 4, 3, 1, 2   B. 4, 3, 2, 1   C. 3, 1, 2, 4   D. 3, 4, 1, 2   1.____

2.
   1. Community Development Agency
   2. Department of Social Services
   3. Board of Estimate
   4. Bureau of Gas and Electricity

   A. 3, 4, 1, 2   B. 1, 2, 4, 3   C. 2, 1, 3, 4   D. 1, 3, 4, 2   2.____

3.
   1. Dr. Chas. K. Dahlman
   2. F. & A. Delivery Service
   3. Department of Water Supply
   4. Demano Men's Custom Tailors

   A. 1, 2, 3, 4   B. 1, 4, 2, 3   C. 4, 1, 2, 3   D. 4, 1, 3, 2   3.____

4.
   1. 48th Street Theater
   2. Fourteenth Street Day Care Center
   3. Professor A. Cartwright
   4. Albert F. McCarthy

   A. 4, 2, 1, 3   B. 4, 3, 1, 2   C. 3, 2, 1, 4   D. 3, 1, 2, 4   4.____

5.
   1. Frances D'Arcy
   2. Mario L. DelAmato
   3. William H. Diamond
   4. Robert J. DuBarry

   A. 1, 2, 4, 3   B. 2, 1, 3, 4   C. 1, 2, 3, 4   D. 2, 1, 3, 4   5.____

6.
   1. Evelyn H. D'Amelio
   2. Jane R. Bailey
   3. Robert Bailey
   4. Frank Baily

   A. 1, 2, 3, 4   B. 1, 3, 2, 4   C. 2, 3, 4, 1   D. 3, 2, 4, 1   6.____

7.
   1. Department of Markets
   2. Bureau of Handicapped Children
   3. Housing Authority Administration Building
   4. Board of Pharmacy

       7.____

| | A. | 2,1,3,4 | B. | 1,2,4,3 | C. | 1,2,3,4 | D. | 3,2,1,4 | |

8. 1. William A. Shea Stadium   8._____
    2. Rapid Speed Taxi Co.
    3. Harry Stampler's Rotisserie
    4. Wilhelm Albert Shea

| | A. | 2, 3, 4, 1 | B. | 4, 1, 3, 2 | C. | 2, 4, 1, 3 | D. | 3, 4, 1, 2 |

9. 1. Robert S. Aaron, M. D.   2. Mrs. Norma S. Aaron   9._____
    3. Irving I. Aronson   4. Darius P. Aanonsen

| | A. | 1, 2, 3, 4 | B. | 2, 4, 1, 3 | C. | 4, 2, 3, 1 | D. | 4, 2, 1, 3 |

10. 1. The Gamut   2. Gilliar Drug Co., Inc.   10._____
    3. Georgette Cosmetology   4. Great Nock Pharmacy

| | A. | 1, 3, 2, 4 | B. | 3, 1, 4, 2 | C. | 1, 2, 3, 4 | D. | 1, 3, 4, 2 |

_____

KEY (CORRECT ANSWERS)

1. A
2. D
3. B
4. D
5. C

6. D
7. D
8. C
9. D
10. A

_____

TEST 7

DIRECTIONS: Each question consists of four names grouped vertically under four different filing arrangements lettered A, B, C, and D. In each question only one of the four arrangements lists the names in the correct filing order according to the Rules for Alphabetical Filing given before. Read these rules carefully. Then, for each question, select the correct filing arrangement, lettered A, B, C, or D and print in the space at the right the letter of that correct filing arrangement.

SAMPLE QUESTION

Arrangement A	*Arrangement B*	*Arrangement C*	*Arrangement D*
Arnold Robinson	Arthur Roberts	Arnold Robinson	Arthur Roberts
Arthur Roberts	J. B. Robin	Arthur Roberts	James Robin
J. B. Robin	James Robin	James Robin	J. B. Robin
James Robin	Arnold Robinson	J. B. Robin	Arnold Robinson

Since, in this sample, *ARRANGEMENT B* is the only one in which the four names are correctly arranged alphabetically, the answer is B.

1.

Arrangement A	*Arrangement B*
Alice Thompson	Eugene Thompkins
Arnold G. Thomas	Alice Thompson
B. Thomas	Arnold G. Thomas
Eugene Thompkins	B. Thomas
Arrangement C	*Arrangement D*
B. Thomas Arnold	Arnold G. Thomas
G. Thomas	B. Thomas
Eugene Thompkins	Eugene Thompkins
Alice Thompson	Alice Thompson

1.____

2.

Arrangement A	*Arrangement B*
Albert Green	A. B. Green
A. B. Green	Albert Green
Frank E. Green	Frank E. Green
Wm. Greenfield	Wm. Greenfield
Arrangement C	*Arrangement D*
Albert Green	A. B. Green
Wm. Greenfield	Frank E. Green
A. B. Green	Albert Green
Frank E. Green	Wm. Greenfield

2.____

3.

Arrangement A	*Arrangement B*
Steven M. Comte	Steven Le Comte
Robt. Count	Steven M. Comte
Robert B. Count	Robert B. Count
Steven Le Comte	Robt. Count
Arrangement C	*Arrangement D*
Steven M. Comte	Robt. Count
Steven Le Comte	Robert B. Count
Robt. Count	Steven Le Comte
Robert B. Count	Steven M. Comte

3.____

4. *Arrangement A*
   Prof. David Towner
   Miss Edna Tower
   Dr. Frank I. Tower
   Mrs. K. C. Towner
   Arrangement C
   Miss Edna Tower
   Dr. Frank I. Tower
   Prof. David Towner
   Mrs. K. C. Towner

   Arrangement B
   Dr. Frank I. Tower
   Miss Edna Tower
   Mrs. K. C. Towner
   Prof. David Towner
   Arrangement D
   Prof. David Towner
   Mrs. K. C. Towner
   Miss Edna Tower
   Dr. Frank I. Tower

   4._____

5. *Arrangement A*
   The Jane Miller Shop
   Joseph Millard Corp.
   John Muller & Co.
   Jean Mullins, Inc.
   Arrangement C
   The Jane Miller Shop
   Jean Mullins, Inc.
   John Muller & Co.
   Joseph Millard Corp.

   Arrangement B
   Joseph Millard Corp.
   The Jane Miller Shop
   John Muller & Co.
   Jean Mullins, Inc.
   Arrangement D
   Joseph Millard Corp.
   John Muller & Co.
   Jean Mullins, Inc.
   The Jane Miller Shop

   5._____

6. *Arrangement A*
   Anthony Delaney
   A. M. D'Elia
   A. De Landri
   Alfred De Monte
   Arrangement C
   A. De Landri
   A. M. D'Elia
   Alfred De Monte
   Anthony Delaney

   Arrangement B
   Anthony Delaney
   A. De Landri
   A. M. D'Elia
   Alfred De Monte
   Arrangement D
   A. De Landri
   Anthony Delaney
   A. M. D'Elia
   Alfred De Monte

   6._____

7. *Arrangement A*
   D. McAllen
   Lewis McBride
   Doris MacAllister
   Lewis T. Mac Bride
   Arrangement C
   Doris MacAllister
   Lewis T. MacBride
   D. McAllen
   Lewis McBride

   Arrangement B
   D. McAllen
   Doris MacAllister
   Lewis McBride
   Lewis T. MacBride
   Arrangement D
   Doris MacAllister
   D. McAllen
   Lewis T. MacBride
   Lewis McBride

   7._____

8. *Arrangement A*   *Arrangement B*   8.____
   6th Ave. Swim Shop 23rd Street Salon
   The Sky Ski School   The Sky Ski School
   Sport Shoe Store   6th Ave. Swim Shop
   23rd Street Salon   Sport Shoe Store
   Arrangement C   *Arrangement D*
   6th Ave. Swim Shop The Sky Ski School
   Sport Shoe Store   6th Ave. Swim Shop
   The Sky Ski School   Sport Shoe Store
   23rd Street Salon   23rd Street Salon

9. *Arrangement A*   *Arrangement B*   9.____
   Charlotte Stair   C. B. Stare
   C. B. Stare   Charles B. Stare
   Charles B. Stare   Charlotte Stair
   Elaine La Stella   Elaine La Stella
   Arrangement C   *Arrangement D*
   Elaine La Stella   Charles B. Stare
   Charlotte Stair   C. B. Stare
   C. B. Stare   Charlotte Stair
   Charles B. Stare   Elaine La Stella

10. *Arrangement A*   *Arrangement B*   10.____
    John O'Farrell Corp. Finest Glass Co.
    Finest Glass Co.   4th Guarantee Bank
    George Fraser Co.   George Fraser Co.
    4th Guarantee Bank John O'Farrell Corp.
    Arrangement C   *Arrangement D*
    John O'Farrell Corp. Finest Glass Co.
    Finest Glass Co.   George Fraser Co.
    4th Guarantee Bank John O'Farrell Corp.
    George Fraser Co.   4th Guarantee Bank

KEY (CORRECT ANSWERS)

1. D
2. B
3. A
4. C
5. B

6. D
7. C
8. A
9. C
10. B

TEST 8

DIRECTIONS: Same as for Test 7.

Arrangement A	Arrangement B	Arrangement C	
1. R. B. Stevens Chas. Stevenson Robert Stevens,Sr. Alfred T. Stevens	Alfred T. Stevens R. B. Stevens Robert Stevens,Sr. Chas. Stevenson	R. B. Stevens Robert Stevens,Sr. Alfred T. Stevens Chas. Stevenson	1.____
2. Mr. A. T. Breen Dr. Otis C. Breen Amelia K.Brewington John Brewington	John Brewington Amelia K.Brewington Dr. Otis C. Breen Mr. A. T. Breen	Dr. Otis C. Breen Mr. A. T. Breen John Brewington Amelia K.Brewington	2.____
3. J. Murphy J. J. Murphy John Murphy John J. Murphy	John Murphy John J. Murphy J. Murphy J. J. Murphy	J. Murphy John Murphy J. J. Murphy John J. Murphy	3.____
4. Anthony DiBuono George Burns,Sr. Geo. T. Burns,Jr. Alan J. Byrnes	Geo. T. Burns,Jr. George Burns,Sr. Anthony DiBuono Alan J. Byrnes	George Burns,Sr. Geo. T. Burns, Jr. Alan J. Byrnes Anthony DiBuono	4.____
5. James Macauley Frank A. McLowery Francis MacLaughry Bernard J. MacMahon	James Macauley Francis MacLoughry Bernard J. MacMahon Frank A. McLowery	Bernard J. MacMahon Francis MacLaughry Frank A. McLowery James Macauley	5.____
6. A.J. DiBartolo,Sr. A. P. DiBartolo J. A. Bartolo Anthony J. Bartolo	J. A. Bartolo Anthony J. Bartolo A. P. DiBartolo A. J. DiBartolo,Sr.	Anthony J. Bartolo J. A. Bartolo A. J. DiBartolo, Sr. A. P. DiBartolo	6.____
7. Edward Holmes Corp. Hillside Trust Corp Standard Insurance Co. The Industrial Surety Co.	Edward Holmes Corp. Hillside Trust Corp. The Industrial Surety Co. Standard Insurance Co.	Hillside TrustCorp. Edward Holmes Corp. The Industrial Surety Co. Standard InsuranceCo.	7.____
8. Cooperative Credit Co. Chas. Cooke Chemical Corp. John Fuller Baking Co. 4th Avenue Express Co.	Chas. Cooke Chemical Corp. Cooperative Credit Co. 4th Avenue Express Co. John Fuller Baking Co.	4th Avenue Express Co. John Fuller Baking Co. Chas. Cooke Chemical Corp. Cooperative CreditCo.	8.____

9. Mr. R. McDaniels
    Robert Darling, Jr.
    F. L. Ramsey
    Charles DeRhone

    F. L. Ramsey
    Mr. R. McDaniels
    Charles DeRhone
    Robert Darling, Jr.

    Robert Darling, Jr. Charles
    DeRhone
    Mr. R. McDaniels
    F. L. Ramsey

    9._____

10. New York Omnibus Corp.
    New York Shipping Co.
    Nova Scotia Canning Co.
    John J. O'Brien Co.

    John J. O'Brien Co.
    New York Omnibus Corp.
    New York Shipping Co.
    Nova Scotia Caning Co.

    Nova Scotia Canning Co.
    John J. O'Brien Co.
    New York Omnibus Corp.
    New York Shipping Co.

    10._____

KEY (CORRECT ANSWERS)

1. B
2. A
3. A
4. C
5. B

6. C
7. C
8. B
9. C
10. A

TEST 9

DIRECTIONS: Each question consists of a group of names. Consider each group of names as a unit. Determine in what position the name printed in *ITALICS* would be if the names in the group were *CORRECTLY* arranged in alphabetical order. If the name in *ITALICS* should be first, print the letter A; if second, print the letter B; if third, print the letter C; if fourth, print the letter D; and if fifth, print the letter E. *PRINT THE LETTER OF THE CORRECT ANSWER IN THE SPACE AT THE RIGHT.*

SAMPLE QUESTION

J. W. Martin	2
James E. Martin	4
J. Martin	1
George Martins	5
James Martin	3

1. Albert Brown
   James Borenstein
   Frieda Albrecht
   Samuel Brown
   George Appelman

   1.____

2. James Ryan
   Francis Ryan
   Wm. Roanan
   Frances S. Ryan
   Francis P. Ryan

   2.____

3. Norman Fitzgibbons
   Charles F. Franklin
   Jas. Fitzgerald
   Andrew Fitzsimmons
   James P. Fitzgerald

   3.____

4. Hugh F. Martenson
   A. S. Martinson
   Albert Martinsen
   Albert S. Martinson
   M. Martanson

   4.____

5. Aaron M. Michelson
   Samuel Michels
   Arthur L. Michaelson, Sr.
   John Michell
   Daniel Michelsohn

   5.____

6. *Chas. R. Connolly*
   Frank Conlon
   Charles S. Connolly
   Abraham Cohen
   Chas. Conolly

6.____

7. James McCormack
   Ruth MacNamara
   Kathryn McGillicuddy
   Frances Mason
   Arthur MacAdams

7.____

8. Dr. Francis Karell
   John Joseph Karelsen,
   Jr. John J.Karelsen,Sr.
   Mrs. Jeanette Kelly
   Estelle Karel

8.____

9. *The 5th Ave. Bus Co.*
   The Baltimore and Ohio Railroad
   3rd Ave. Elevated Co.
   Pennsylvania Railroad
   The 4th Ave. Trolley Line

9.____

10. Murray B. Cunitz
    Cunningham Duct Cleaning Corp.
    James A. Cunninghame
    Jason M. Cuomor
    Talmadge L. Cummings

10.____

KEY (CORRECT ANSWERS)

1.	E
2.	D
3.	A
4.	E
5.	D
6.	C
7.	C
8.	D
9.	B
10.	C

TEST 10

DIRECTIONS: A supervisor who is responsible for the proper maintenance and operation of the filing system in an office of a depart-ment should be able to instruct and guide his subordinates in the correct filing of office records. The following ques-tions,1 through 10, are designed to determine whether you can interpret and follow a prescribed filing procedure. These questions should be answered SOLELY on the basis of the fil-ing instructions which follow.

FILING INSTRUCTIONS FOR PERSONNEL DIVISION
DEPARTMENT X

The filing system of this division consists of three separate files, namely: (1) Employee File, (2) Subject File, (3) Correspondence File.

Employee File

This file contains a folder for each person currently employed in the department. Each report, memorandum, and letter which has been received from an official or employee of the department and which pertions to one employee only should be placed in the Employee File folder of the employee with whom the communication is concerned. (Note: This filing proce-dure also applies to a communication from a staff member who writes on a matter which con-cerns himself only.)

Subject File

Reports and memoranda originating in the department and dealing with personnel mat-ters affecting the entire staff or certain categories or groups of employees should be placed in the Subject File under the appropriate subject headings. The materials in this file are subdi-vided under the following five subject headings:

(1) Classification -- includes material on job analysis, change of title, reclassifica-tion of positions, etc.

(2) Employment -- includes material on appointment, promotion, re-instatement, and transfer.

(3) Health and Safety -- includes material dealing chiefly with the health and safety of employees.

(4) Staff Regulations -- includes material pertaining to rules and regulations gov-erning such working conditions as hours of work, lateness, vacation, leave of absence, etc.

(5) Training -- includes all material relating to employee training.

Correspondence File

All correspondence received from outside agencies, both public and private, and from persons outside the department, should be placed in the Correspondence File and cross ref-erenced as follows:

(1) When letters from outside agencies or persons relate to one or more employees currently employed in the department, a cross reference sheet should be placed in the Employee File folder of each employee mentioned.

(2) When letters from outside agencies or persons do not mention a specific employee or specific employees of the department, a cross reference sheet should be placed in the Subject File under the appropriate subject heading.

Questions 1-10 describe communications which have been received and acted upon by the Personnel Division of Department X, and which must be filed in accordance with the Filing Instructions for the Personnel Division.

The following filing operations may be performed in accordance with the above filing instructions:

- (A) Place in Employee File
- (B) Place in Subject File under Classification
- (C) Place in Subject File tinder Employment
- (D) Place in Subject File under Health and Safety
- (E) Place in Subject File under Staff Regulations
- (F) Place in Subject File under Training
- (G) Place in Correspondence File and cross reference in Employee File
- (H) Place in Correspondence File and cross reference in Subject File under Classification
- (I) Place in Correspondence File and cross reference in Subject File under Employment
- (J) Place in Correspondence File and cross reference in Subject File under Health and Safety
- (K) Place in Correspondence File and cross reference in Subject File under Staff Regulations
- (L) Place in Correspondence File and cross reference in Subject File under Training

DIRECTIONS: Examine each of questions 1 through 10 carefully. Then, in the space at the right, *print* the capital letter preceding the one of the filing operations listed above which MOST accurately carries out the Filing Instructions for the Personnel Division.

SAMPLE: A Clerk, Grade 2, in the department has sent in a memorandum requesting information regarding the amount of vacation due him.
The CORRECT answer is A.

1. Mr. Clark, a Clerk, Grade 5, has submitted an intradepartmental memorandum that the titles of all Clerks, Grade 5, in the department be changed to Administrative Assistant.　　1.＿＿＿＿

2. The secretary to the department has issued a staff order revising the schedule of Saturday work from a one-in-two to a one-in-four schedule.　　2.＿＿＿＿

3. The personnel officer of another agency has requested the printed transcripts of an in-service course recently conducted by the department.　　3.＿＿＿＿

4. Mary Smith, a secretary to one of the division chiefs, has sent in a request for a maternity leave of absence to begin on April 1 of this year and to terminate on March 31 of next year.　　4.＿＿＿＿

5. A letter has been received from a civic organization stating that they would like to know how many employees were promoted in the department during the last fiscal year.　　5.＿＿＿＿

6. The attorney for a municipal employees' organization has requested permission to represent Mr.James Roe, a departmental employee who is being brought up on charges of violating departmental regulations.　　6.＿＿＿＿

7. A letter has been received from Mr. Wright, a salesman for a paper company, who complains that Miss Jones, an information clerk in the department, has been rude and impertinent and has refused to give him information which should be available to the public.　　7.＿＿＿＿

8. Helen Brown, a graduate of Commercial High School, has sent a letter inquiring about an appointment as a provisional typist.   8.____

9. The National Office Managers' Society has sent a request to the department for information on its policies on tardiness and absenteeism.   9.____

10. A memorandum has been received from a division chief who states that employees in his unit have complained that their rest room is in a very unsanitary condition.   10.____

_____

KEY (CORRECT ANSWERS)

1. B
2. E
3. L
4. A
5. I

6. G
7. G
8. I
9. K
10. D

_____

INTERPRETING STATISTICAL DATA GRAPHS, CHARTS AND TABLES

EXAMINATION SECTION
TEST 1

DIRECTIONS: Each question or incomplete statement is followed by several suggested answers or completions. Select the one that BEST answers the question or completes the statement. *PRINT THE LETTER OF THE CORRECT ANSWER IN THE SPACE AT THE RIGHT.*

Questions 1-12.

DIRECTIONS: Questions 1 through 12 are to be answered SOLELY on the basis of the information given in the graph and chart below.

ENROLLMENT IN POSTGRADUATE STUDIES

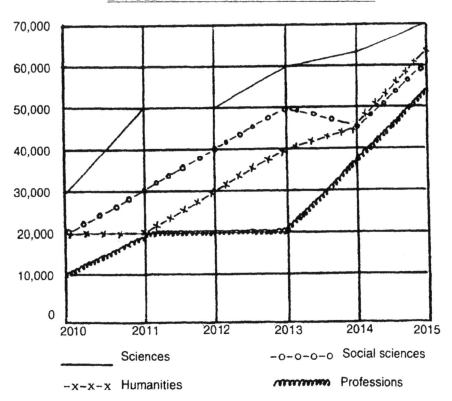

Fields	Subdivsions	2014	2015
Sciences	Math	10,000	12,000
	Physical science	22,000	24,000
	Behavioral science	32,000	35,000
Humanities	Literature	26,000	34,000
	Philosophy	6,000	8,000
	Religion	4,000	6,000
	Arts	10,000	16,000
Social sciences	History	36,000	46,000
	Sociology	8,000	14,000
Professions	Law	2,000	2,000
	Medicine	6,000	8,000
	Business	30,000	44,000

1. The number of students enrolled in the social sciences and in the humanities was the same in

   1.____

  A. 2012 and 2014   B. 2010 and 2014
  C. 2014 and 2015   D. 2011 and 2014

2. A comparison of the enrollment of students in the various postgraduate studies shows that in every year from 2010 through 2015, there were MORE students enrolled in the _____ than in the _____.

   2.____

  A. professions; sciences
  B. humanities; professions
  C. social sciencies; professions
  D. humanities; sciences

3. The number of students enrolled in the humanities was GREATER than the number of students enrolled in the professions by the same amount in _____ of the years.

   3.____

  A. two   B. three   C. four   D. five

4. The one field of postgraduate study to show a DECREASE in enrollment in one year compared to the year immediately preceding is

   4.____

  A. humanities   B. sciences
  C. professions   D. social sciences

5. If the proportion of arts students to all humanities students was the same in 2012 as in 2015, then the number of arts students in 2012 was

   5.____

  A. 7,500   B. 13,000   C. 15,000   D. 5,000

6. In which field of postgraduate study did enrollment INCREASE by 20 percent from 2012 to 2013?   6._____

    A. Humanities   B. Professions
    C. Sciences   D. Social sciences

7. The GREATEST increase in overall enrollment took place between   7._____

    A. 2010 and 2011   B. 2012 and 2013
    C. 2013 and 2014   D. 2013 and 2015

8. Between 2012 and 2015, the combined enrollment of the sciences and social sciences INCREASED by   8._____

    A. 40,000   B. 48,000   C. 50,000   D. 54,000

9. If the enrollment in the social sciences had decreased from 2014 to 2015 at the same rate as from 2013 to 2014, then the social science enrollment in 2015 would have differed from the humanities enrollment in 2015 MOST NEARLY by   9._____

    A. 6,000   B. 8,000   C. 12,000   D. 22,000

10. In the humanities, the GREATEST percentage increase in enrollment from 2014 to 2015 was in   10._____

    A. literature   B. philosophy
    C. religion   D. arts

11. If the proportion of behavioral science students to the total number of students in the sciences was the same in 2011 as in 2014, then the increase in behavioral science enrollment from 2011 to 2015 was   11._____

    A. 5,000   B. 7,000   C. 10,000   D. 14,000

12. If enrollment in the professions increased at the same rate from 2015 to 2016 as from 2014 to 2015, the enrollment in the professions in 2001 would be MOST NEARLY   12._____

    A. 85,000   B. 75,000   C. 60,000   D. 55,000

KEY (CORRECT ANSWERS)

1.	B		6.	C
2.	C		7.	D
3.	B		8.	A
4.	D		9.	D
5.	A		10.	D

11.	C
12.	B

TEST 2

DIRECTIONS: Questions 1 through 5 involve calculations of annual grade averages for college students who have just completed their junior year. These averages are to be based on the following table showing the number of credit hours for each student during the year at each of the grade levels: A, B, C, D, and F. How these letter grades may be translated into numerical grades is indicated in the first column of the table.

| Grade | Credit Hours - Junior Year | | | | | |
Value	King	Lewis	Martin	Nonkin	Ottly	Perry
A = 95	12	12	9	15	6	3
B = 85	9	12	9	12	18	6
C = 75	6	6	9	3	3	21
D = 65	3	3	3	3	—	—
F = 0	—	—	3	—	—	—

Calculating a grade average for an individual student is a four-step process:

   I.   Multiply each grade value by the number of credit hours for which the student received that grade.
   II. Add these multiplication products for each student.
  III. Add the student's total credit hours.
  IV. Divide the multiplication product total by the total number of credit hours.
   V. Round the result, if there is a decimal place, to the nearest whole number. A number ending in .5 would be rounded to the next higher number.

EXAMPLE:

Using student King's grades as an example, his grade average can be calculated by going through the following four steps:

   I. 95 x 12 = 1140   III. 12
      85 x 9 = 765   9
      75 x 6 = 450   6
      65 x 3 = 195   3
       0 x 0 =   0   0
                       30 TOTAL credit hours

   II. TOTAL = 2550   IV. Divide 2550 by 30: $\dfrac{2550}{30}$ = 85.

King's grade average is 85

1. The grade average of Lewis is   1.____

    A. 83   B. 84   C. 85   D. 86

2. The grade average of Martin is   2.____

    A. 72   B. 73   C. 74   D. 75

3. The grade average of Nonkin is

    A. 85   B. 86   C. 87   D. 88

3.____

4. Student Ottly must attain a grade average of 90 in each of his years in college to be accepted into the graduate school of his choice.
If, in summer school during his junior year, he takes two three-credit courses and receives a grade of 95 in each one, his grade average for his junior year will then be MOST NEARLY

    A. 87   B. 88   C. 89   D. 90

4.____

5. If Perry takes an additional three-credit course during the year and receives a grade of 95, his grade average will be increased to APPROXIMATELY

    A. 79   B. 80   C. 81   D. 82

5.____

KEY (CORRECT ANSWERS)

    1. C
    2. D
    3. C
    4. B
    5. B

TEST 3

DIRECTIONS: Questions 1 through 5 are to be answered SOLELY on the basis of the following information and chart.

The following table gives pertinent data for six different applicants with regard to:

Grade averages, which are expressed on a scale running from 0 (low) to 4 (high); Scores on qualifying test, which run from 200 (low) to 800 (high); Related work experience, which is expressed in number of months; Personal references, which are rated from 1 (low) to 5 (high).

Applicant	Grade Average	Test Score	Work Experience	Reference
Jones	2.2	620	24	3
Perez	3.5	650	0	5
Lowitz	3.2	420	2	4
Uncker	2.1	710	15	2
Farrow	2.8	560	0	3
Shapiro	3.0	560	12	4

An administrative assistant is in charge of the initial screening process for the program. This process requires classifying applicants into the following four groups:

A.   SUPERIOR CANDIDATES. Unless the personal reference rating is lower than 3, all applicants with grade averages of 3.0 or higher and test scores of 600 or higher are classified as superior candidates.

B.   GOOD CANDIDATES. Unless the personal reference rating is lower than 3, all applicants with one of the following combinations of grade averages and test scores are classified as good candidates:

1. Grade average of 2.5 to 2.9 and test score of 600 or higher;
2. Grade average of 3.0 or higher and test score of 550 to 599.

C.   POSSIBLE CANDIDATES. Applicants with one of the following combinations of qualifications are classified as possible candidates:

1. Grade average of 2.5 to 2.9 and test score of 550 to 599 and a personal reference rating of 3 or higher;
2. Grade average of 2.0 to 2.4 and test score of 500 or higher and at least 21 months' work experience and a personal reference rating of 3 or higher;
3. A combination of grade average and test score that would otherwise qualify as *superior* or *good* but a personal reference score lower than 3.

D.   REJECTED CANDIDATES. Applicants who do not fall in any of the above groups are to be rejected.

EXAMPLE:

Jones' grade average of 2.2 does not meet the standard for either a superior candidate (grade average must be 3.0-or higher) or a good candidate (grade average must be 2.5 to 2.9). Grade average of 2.2 does not qualify Jones as a possible candidate if Jones has a test score of 500 or higher, at least 21 months' work experience, and a personal reference rating of 3 or higher. Since Jones has a test score of 620, 24 months' work experience, and a reference rating of 3, Jones is a possible candidate. The answer is C.

Answer Questions 1 through 5 as explained above, indicating for each whether the applicant should be classified as a

A. superior candidate   B. good candidate
C. possible candidate   D. rejected candidate

1. Perez   1._____

2. Lowitz   2._____

3. Uncker   3._____

4. Farrow   4._____

5. Shapiro   5._____

KEY (CORRECT ANSWERS)

1. A
2. D
3. D
4. C
5. B

READING COMPREHENSION
UNDERSTANDING AND INTERPRETING WRITTEN MATERIAL
EXAMINATION SECTION
TEST 1

DIRECTIONS: Each question or incomplete statement is followed by several suggested answers or completions. Select the one that BEST answers the question or completes the statement. *PRINT THE LETTER OF THE CORRECT ANSWER IN THE SPACE AT THE RIGHT.*

Questions 1-3.

DIRECTIONS: Questions 1 through 3 are to be answered SOLELY on the basis of the following paragraph.

Every organization needs a systematic method of checking its operations as a means to increase efficiency and promote economy. Many successful private firms have instituted a system of audits or internal inspections to accomplish these ends. Law enforcement organizations, which have an extremely important service to *sell,* should be no less zealous in developing efficiency and economy in their operations. Periodic, organized, and systematic inspections are one means of promoting the achievement of these objectives. The necessity of an organized inspection system is perhaps greatest in those law enforcement groups which have grown to such a size that the principal officer can no longer personally supervise or be cognizant of every action taken. Smooth and effective operation demands that the head of the organization have at hand some tool with which he can study and enforce general policies and procedures and also direct compliance with day-to-day orders, most of which are put into execution outside his sight and hearing. A good inspection system can serve as that tool.

1. The central thought of the above paragraph is that a system of inspections within a police department

    A. is unnecessary for a department in which the principal officer can personally supervise all official actions taken

    B. should be instituted at the first indication that there is any deterioration in job performance by the force

    C. should be decentralized and administered by first-line supervisory officers

    D. is an important aid to the police administrator in the accomplishment of law enforcement objectives

1.____

2. The MOST accurate of the following statements concerning the need for an organized inspection system in a law enforcement organization is: It is

    A. never needed in an organization of small size where the principal officer can give personal supervision

    B. most needed where the size of the organization prevents direct supervision by the principal officer

    C. more needed in law enforcement organizations than in private firms

    D. especially needed in an organization about to embark upon a needed expansion of services

2.____

3. According to the above paragraph, the head of the police organization utilizes the internal inspection system
3._____

   A. as a tool which must be constantly re-examined in the light of changing demands for police service
   B. as an administrative technique to increase efficiency and promote economy
   C. by personally visiting those areas of police operation which are outside his sight and hearing
   D. to augment the control of local commanders over detailed field operations

Questions 4-10.

DIRECTIONS: Questions 4 through 10 are to be answered SOLELY on the basis of the following passage.

Job evaluation and job rating systems are intended to introduce scientific procedures. Any type of approach, when properly used, will give satisfactory results. The Point System, when properly validated by actual use, is more likely to be suitable for general use than the ranking system. In many aspects, the Factor Comparison Plan is a point system tied to money values. Of course, there may be another system that combines the ranking system with the point system, especially during the initial stages of the development of the program. After the program has been in use for some time, the tendency is to drop off the ranking phase and continue the use of the point system.

In the ranking system of rating of jobs, every job within the plant is arranged in some order, either from the one with the simplest qualifications to the one with maximum requirements, or in the reverse order. This system should be preceded by careful job analysis and the writing of accurate job descriptions before the rating process is undertaken. It is possible, of course, to take the jobs as they are found in the business enterprise and use the names as they are without any attempt at standardization, and merely rank them according to the general over-all impression of the raters. Such a procedure is certain to fall short of what may reasonably be expected of job rating. Another procedure that is in reality merely a modification of the simple rating described above is to establish a series of grades or zones and arrange all the jobs in the plant into groups within these grades and zones. The practice in most common use is to arrange all the jobs in the plant according to their requirements by rating them and then to establish the classifications or groups.

The actual ranking of jobs may be done by one individual, several individuals, or a committee. If several individuals are working independently on the task, it will usually be found that, in general, they agree but that their rankings vary in certain details. A conference between the individuals, with each person giving his reasons why he rated one way or another, usually produces agreement. The detailed job descriptions are particularly helpful when there is disagreement among raters as to the rating of certain jobs. It is not only possible but desirable to have workers participate in the construction of the job description and in rating the job.

4. The MAIN theme of this passage is
4._____

   A. the elimination of bias in job rating
   B. the rating of jobs by the ranking system

C.   the need for accuracy in allocating points in the point system
D.   pitfalls to avoid in selecting key jobs in the Factor Comparison Plan

5.   The ranking system of rating jobs consists MAINLY of   5.____

A.   attaching a point value to each ratable factor of each job prior to establishing an
     equitable pay scale
B.   arranging every job in the organization in descending order and then following this
     up with a job analysis of the key jobs
C.   preparing accurate job descriptions after a job analysis and then arranging all jobs
     either in ascending or descending order based on job requirements
D.   arbitrarily establishing a hierarchy of job classes and grades and then fitting each
     job into a specific class and grade based on the opinions of unit supervisors

6.   The above passage states that the system of classifying jobs MOST used in an organiza-   6.____
     tion is to

A.   organize all jobs in the organization in accordance with their requirements and
     then create categories or clusters of jobs
B.   classify all jobs in the organization according to the titles and rank by which they
     are currently known in the organization
C.   establish a pre-arranged series of grades or zones and then fit
D.   all jobs into one of the grades or zones
E.   determine the salary currently being paid for each job and then rank the jobs in
     order according to salary

7.   According to the above passage, experience has shown that when a group of raters is   7.____
     assigned to the job evaluation task and each individual rates independently of the others,
     the raters GENERALLY

A.   agree with respect to all aspects of their rankings
B.   disagree with respect to all or nearly all aspects of the rankings
C.   disagree on overall ratings, but agree on specific rating factors
D.   agree on overall rankings, but have some variance in some details

8.   The above passage states that the use of a detailed job description is of SPECIAL value   8.____
     when

A.   employees of an organization have participated in the preliminary step involved in
     actual preparation of the job description
B.   labor representatives are not participating in ranking of the jobs
C.   an individual rater who is unsure of himself is ranking the jobs
D.   a group of raters is having difficulty reaching unanimity with respect to ranking a
     certain job

9.   A comparison of the various rating systems as described in the above passage shows   9.____
     that

A.   the ranking system is not as appropriate for general use as a properly validated
     point system
B.   the point system is the same as the Factor Comparison Plan except that it places
     greater emphasis on money

C. no system is capable of combining the point system and the Factor Comparison Plan
D. the point system will be discontinued last when used in combination with the Factor Comparison System

10. The above passage implies that the PRINCIPAL reason for creating job evaluation and rating systems was to help

    10.____

    A. overcome union opposition to existing salary plans
    B. base wage determination on a more objective and orderly foundation
    C. eliminate personal bias on the part of the trained scientific job evaluators
    D. management determine if it was overpricing the various jobs in the organizational hierarchy

Questions 11-13.

DIRECTIONS: Questions 11 through 13 are to be answered SOLELY on the basis of the following paragraph.

The common sense character of the merit system seems so natural to most Americans that many people wonder why it should ever have been inoperative. After all, the American economic system, the most phenomenal the world has ever known, is also founded on a rugged selective process which emphasizes the personal qualities of capacity, industriousness, and productivity. The criteria may not have always been appropriate and competition has not always been fair, but competition there was, and the responsibilities and the rewards – with exceptions, of course – have gone to those who could measure up in terms of intelligence, knowledge, or perseverance. This has been true not only in the economic area, in the money-making process, but also in achievement in the professions and other walks of life.

11. According to the above paragraph, economic rewards in the United States have

    11.____

    A. always been based on appropriate, fair criteria
    B. only recently been based on a competitive system
    C. not gone to people who compete too ruggedly
    D. usually gone to those people with intelligence, knowledge, and perseverance

12. According to the above passage, a merit system is

    12.____

    A. an unfair criterion on which to base rewards
    B. unnatural to anyone who is not American
    C. based only on common sense
    D. based on the same principles as the American economic system

13. According to the above passage, it is MOST accurate to say that

    13.____

    A. the United States has always had a civil service merit system
    B. civil service employees are very rugged
    C. the American economic system has always been based on a merit objective
    D. competition is unique to the American way of life

Questions 14-15.

DIRECTIONS: Questions 14 and 15 are to be answered SOLELY on the basis of the following paragraph.

In-basket tests are often used to assess managerial potential. The exercise consists of a set of papers that would be likely to be found in the in-basket of an administrator or manager at any given time, and requires the individuals participating in the examination to indicate how they would dispose of each item found in the in-basket. In order to handle the in-basket effectively, they must successfully manage their time, refer and assign some work to subordinates, juggle potentially conflicting appointments and meetings, and arrange for follow-up of problems generated by the items in the in-basket. In other words, the in-basket test is attempting to evaluate the participants' abilities to organize their work, set priorities, delegate, control, and make decisions.

14.   According to the above paragraph, to succeed in an in-basket test, an administrator must   14.____

    A.   be able to read very quickly
    B.   have a great deal of technical knowledge
    C.   know when to delegate work
    D.   arrange a lot of appointments and meetings

15.   According to the above paragraph, all of the following abilities are indications of managerial potential EXCEPT the ability to   15.____

    A.   organize and control   B.   manage time
    C.   write effective reports   D.   make appropriate decisions

Questions 16-19.

DIRECTIONS: Questions 16 through 19 are to be answered SOLELY on the basis of the following paragraph.

A personnel researcher has at his disposal various approaches for obtaining information, analyzing it, and arriving at conclusions that have value in predicting and affecting the behavior of people at work. The type of method to be used depends on such factors as the nature of the research problem, the available data, and the attitudes of those people being studied to the various kinds of approaches. While the experimental approach, with its use of control groups, is the most refined type of study, there are others that are often found useful in personnel research. Surveys, in which the researcher obtains facts on a problem from a variety of sources, are employed in research on wages, fringe benefits, and labor relations. Historical studies are used to trace the development of problems in order to understand them better and to isolate possible causative factors. Case studies are generally developed to explore all the details of a particular problem that is representative of other similar problems. A researcher chooses the most appropriate form of study for the problem he is investigating. He should recognize, however, that the experimental method, commonly referred to as the scientific method, if used validly and reliably, gives the most conclusive results.

16.   The above paragraph discusses several approaches used to obtain information on particular problems. Which of the following may be MOST reasonably concluded from the paragraph?   16.____
    A(n)

A. historical study cannot determine causative factors
B. survey is often used in research on fringe benefits
C. case study is usually used to explore a problem that is unique and unrelated to other problems
D. experimental study is used when the scientific approach to a problem fails

17. According to the above paragraph, all of the following are factors that may determine the type of approach a researcher uses EXCEPT   17.____

    A. the attitudes of people toward being used in control groups
    B. the number of available sources
    C. his desire to isolate possible causative factors
    D. the degree of accuracy he requires

18. The words *scientific method*, as used in the last sentence of the above paragraph, refer to a type of study which, according to the above paragraph   18.____

    A. uses a variety of sources
    B. traces the development of problems
    C. uses control groups
    D. analyzes the details of a representative problem

19. Which of the following can be MOST reasonably concluded from the above paragraph? In obtaining and analyzing information on a particular problem, a researcher employs the method which is the   19.____

    A. most accurate   B. most suitable
    C. least expensive   D. least time-consuming

Questions 20-25.

DIRECTIONS: Questions 20 through 25 are to be answered SOLELY on the basis of the following passage.

The quality of the voice of a worker is an important factor in conveying to clients and co-workers his attitude and, to some degree, his character. The human voice, when not consciously disguised, may reflect a person's mood, temper, and personality. It has been shown in several experiments that certain character traits can be assessed with better than chance accuracy through listening to the voice of an unknown person who cannot be seen.

Since one of the objectives of the worker is to put clients at ease and to present an encouraging and comfortable atmosphere, a harsh, shrill, or loud voice could have a negative effect. A client who displays emotions of anger or resentment would probably be provoked even further by a caustic tone. In a face-to-face situation, an unpleasant voice may be compensated for, to some degree, by a concerned and kind facial expression. However, when one speaks on the telephone, the expression on one's face cannot be seen by the listener. A supervising clerk who wishes to represent himself effectively to clients should try to eliminate as many faults as possible in striving to develop desirable voice qualities.

20. If a worker uses a sarcastic tone while interviewing a resentful client, the client, according to the above passage, would MOST likely   20.____

    A. avoid the face-to-face situation
    B. be ashamed of his behavior
    C. become more resentful
    D. be provoked to violence

21. According to the passage, experiments comparing voice and character traits have demonstrated that   21.____

    A. prospects for improving an unpleasant voice through training are better than chance
    B. the voice can be altered to project many different psychological characteristics
    C. the quality of the human voice reveals more about the speaker than his words do
    D. the speaker's voice tells the hearer something about the speaker's personality

22. Which of the following, according to the above passage, is a person's voice MOST likely to reveal?   22.____
His

    A. prejudices   B. intelligence
    C. social awareness   D. temperament

23. It may be MOST reasonably concluded from the above passage that an interested and sympathetic expression on the face of a worker   23.____

    A. may induce a client to feel certain he will receive welfare benefits
    B. will eliminate the need for pleasant vocal qualities in the interviewer
    C. may help to make up for an unpleasant voice in the interviewer
    D. is desirable as the interviewer speaks on the telephone to a client

24. Of the following, the MOST reasonable implication of the above paragraph is that a worker should, when speaking to a client, control and use his voice to   24.____

    A. simulate a feeling of interest in the problems of the client
    B. express his emotions directly and adequately
    C. help produce in the client a sense of comfort and security
    D. reflect his own true personality

25. It may be concluded from the above passage that the PARTICULAR reason for a worker to pay special attention to modulating her voice when talking on the phone to a client is that, during a telephone conversation,   25.____

    A. there is a necessity to compensate for the way in which a telephone distorts the voice
    B. the voice of the worker is a reflection of her mood and character
    C. the client can react only on the basis of the voice and words she hears
    D. the client may have difficulty getting a clear under-standing over the telephone

149

KEY (CORRECT ANSWERS)

1. D	11. D
2. B	12. D
3. B	13. C
4. B	14. C
5. C	15. C
6. A	16. B
7. D	17. D
8. D	18. C
9. A	19. B
10. B	20. C

21. D
22. D
23. C
24. C
25. C

———

TEST 2

Questions 1-3.

DIRECTIONS: Questions 1 through 3 are to be answered SOLELY on the basis of the follow-ing paragraph.

Suppose you are given the job of printing, collating, and stapling 8,000 copies of a ten-page booklet as soon as possible. You have available one photo-offset machine, a collator with an automatic stapler, and the personnel to operate these machines. All will be available for however long the job takes to complete. The photo-offset machine prints 5,000 impres-sions an hour, and it takes about 15 minutes to set up a plate. The collator, including time for insertion of pages and stapling, can process about 2,000 booklets an hour. (Answers should be based on the assumption that there are no breakdowns or delays.)

1. Assuming that all the printing is finished before the collating is started, if the job is given   1.____
   to you late Monday and your section can begin work the next day and is able to devote
   seven hours a day, Monday through Friday, to the job until it is finished, what is the BEST
   estimate of when the job will be finished?

   A. Wednesday afternoon of the same week
   B. Thursday morning of the same week
   C. Friday morning of the same week
   D. Monday morning of the next week

2. An operator suggests to you that instead of completing all the printing and then begin-   2.____
   ning collating and stapling, you first print all the pages for 4,000 booklets, so that they
   can be collated and stapled while the last 4,000 booklets are being printed.
   If you accepted this suggestion, the job would be completed

   A. sooner but would require more man-hours
   B. at the same time using either method
   C. later and would require more man-hours
   D. sooner but there would be more wear and tear on the plates

3. Assume that you have the same assignment and equipment as described above, but   3.____
   16,000 copies of the booklet are needed instead of 8,000.
   If you decided to print 8,000 complete booklets, then collate and staple them while you
   started printing the next 8,000 booklets, which of the following statements would
   MOST accurately describe the relationship between this new method and your original
   method of printing all the booklets at one time, and then collating and stapling them?
   The

   A. job would be completed at the same time regardless of the method used
   B. new method would result in the job's being completed 3 1/2 hours earlier
   C. original method would result in the job's being completed an hour later
   D. new method would result in the job's being completed 1 1/2 hours earlier.

Questions 4-6.

DIRECTIONS: Questions 4 through 6 are to be answered SOLELY on the basis of the follow-ing passage.

When using words like company, association, council, committee, and board in place of the full official name, the writer should not capitalize these short forms unless he intends them to invoke the full force of the institution's authority. In legal contracts, in minutes, or in formal correspondence where one is speaking formally and officially on behalf of the company, the term Company is usually capitalized, but in ordinary usage, where it is not essential to load the short form with this significance, capitalization would be excessive. (Example: The company will have many good openings for graduates this June.)

The treatment recommended for short forms of place names is essentially the same as that recommended for short forms of organizational names. In general, we capitalize the full form but not the short form. If Park Avenue is referred to in one sentence, then the *avenue* is sufficient in subsequent references. The same is true with words like building, hotel, station, and airport, which are capitalized when part of a proper name changed (Pan Am Building, Hotel Plaza, Union Station, O'Hare Airport), but are simply lower-cased when replacing these specific names.

4. The above passage states that USUALLY the short forms of names of organizations   4._____

    A. and places should not be capitalized
    B. and places should be capitalized
    C. should not be capitalized, but the short forms of names of places should be capitalized
    D. should be capitalized, but the short forms of names of places should not be capitalized

5. The above passage states that in legal contracts, in minutes, and in formal correspon-   5._____
dence, the short forms of names of organizations should

    A. usually not be capitalized
    B. usually be capitalized
    C. usually not be used
    D. never be used

6. It can be INFERRED from the above passage that decisions regarding when to capitalize   6._____
certain words

    A. should be left to the discretion of the writer
    B. should be based on generally accepted rules
    C. depend on the total number of words capitalized
    D. are of minor importance

Questions 7-10.

DIRECTIONS: Questions 7 through 10 are to be answered SOLELY on the basis of the following passage.

Use of the systems and procedures approach to office management is revolutionizing the supervision of office work. This approach views an enterprise as an entity which seeks to fulfill.definite objectives. Systems and procedures help to organize repetitive work into a routine, thus reducing the amount of decision making required for its accomplishment. As a result, employees are guided in their efforts and perform only necessary work. Supervisors are relieved of any details of execution and are free to attend to more important work. Establishing work guides which require that identical tasks be performed the same way each time permits standardization of forms, machine operations, work methods, and controls. This approach also reduces the probability of errors. Any error committed is usually discovered quickly because the incorrect work does not meet the requirement of the work guides. Errors are also reduced through work specialization, which allows each employee to become thoroughly proficient in a particular type of work. Such proficiency also tends to improve the morale of the employees.

7. The above passage states that the accuracy of an employee's work is INCREASED by   7.____

    A. using the work specialization approach
    B. employing a probability sample
    C. requiring him to shift at one time into different types of tasks
    D. having his supervisor check each detail of work execution

8. Of the following, which one BEST expresses the main theme of the above passage? The   8.____

    A. advantages and disadvantages of the systems and procedures approach to office management
    B. effectiveness of the systems and procedures approach to office management in developing skills
    C. systems and procedures approach to office management as it relates to office costs
    D. advantages of the systems and procedures approach to office management for supervisors and office workers

9. Work guides are LEAST likely to be used when   9.____

    A. standardized forms are used
    B. a particular office task is distinct and different from all others
    C. identical tasks are to be performed in identical ways
    D. similar work methods are expected from each employee

10. According to the above passage, when an employee makes a work error, it USUALLY   10.____

    A. is quickly corrected by the supervisor
    B. necessitates a change in the work guides
    C. can be detected quickly if work guides are in use
    D. increases the probability of further errors by that employee

Questions 11-12.

DIRECTIONS: Questions 11 and 12 are to be answered SOLELY on the basis of the following passage.

The coordination of the many activities of a large public agency is absolutely essential. Coordination, as an administrative principle, must be distinguished from and is independent of cooperation. Coordination can be of either the horizontal or the vertical type. In large organizations, the objectives of vertical coordination are achieved by the transmission of orders and statements of policy down through the various levels of authority. It is an accepted generalization that the more authoritarian the organization, the more easily may vertical coordination be accomplished. Horizontal coordination is arrived at through staff work, administrative management, and conferences of administrators of equal rank. It is obvious that of the two types of coordination, the vertical kind is more important, for at best horizontal coordination only supplements the coordination effected up and down the line.

11. According to the above passage, the ease with which vertical coordination is achieved in a large agency depends upon 11.____

    A. the extent to which control is firmly exercised from above
    B. the objectives that have been established for the agency
    C. the importance attached by employees to the orders and statements of policy transmitted through the agency
    D. the cooperation obtained at the various levels of authority

12. According to the above passage, 12.____

    A. vertical coordination is dependent for its success upon horizontal coordination
    B. one type of coordination may work in opposition to the other
    C. similar methods may be used to achieve both types of coordination
    D. horizontal coordination is at most an addition to vertical coordination

Questions 13-17.

DIRECTIONS: Questions 13 through 17 are to be answered SOLELY on the basis of the following situation.

Assume that you are a newly appointed supervisor in the same unit in which you have been acting as a provisional for some time. You have in your unit the following workers:

WORKER I - He has always been an efficient worker. In a number of his cases, the clients have recently begun to complain that they cannot manage on the departmental budget.

WORKER II - He has been under selective supervision for some time as an experienced, competent worker. He now begins to be late for his supervisory conferences and to stress how much work he has to do.

WORKER III - He has been making considerable improvement in his ability to handle the details of his job. He now tells you, during an individual conference, that he does not need such close supervision and that he wants to operate more independently. He says that Worker II is always available when he needs a little information or help but, in general, he can manage very well by himself.

WORKER IV - He brings you a complex case for decision as to eligibility. Discussion of the case brings out the fact that he has failed to consider all the available resources adequately but has stressed the family's needs to include every extra item in the budget. This is the third case of a similar nature that this worker has brought to you recently. This worker and Worker I work in adjacent territory and are rather friendly.

In the following questions, select the option that describes the method of dealing with these workers that illustrates BEST supervisory practice.

13. With respect to supervision of Worker I, the assistant supervisor should   13.____

    A. discuss with the worker, in an individual conference, any problems that he may be having due to the increase in the cost of living

    B. plan a group conference for the unit around budgeting, as both Workers I and IV seem to be having budgetary difficulties

    C. discuss with Workers I and IV together the meaning of money as acceptance or rejection to the clients

    D. discuss with Worker I the budgetary data in each case in relation to each client's situation

14. With respect to supervision of Worker II, the supervisor should   14.____

    A. move slowly with this worker and give him time to learn that the supervisor's official appointment has not changed his attitudes or methods of supervision

    B. discuss the worker's change of attitude and ask him to analyze the reasons for his change in behavior

    C. take time to show the worker how he is avoiding his responsibility in the supervisor-worker relationship and that he is resisting supervision

    D. hold an evaluatory conference with the worker and show him how he is taking over responsibilities that are not his by providing supervision for Worker III

15. With respect to supervision of Worker III, the supervisor should discuss with this worker   15.____

    A. why he would rather have supervision from Worker II than from the supervisor

    B. the necessity for further improvement before he can go on selective supervision

    C. an analysis of the improvement that has been made and the extent to which the worker is able to handle the total job for which he is responsible

    D. the responsibility of the supervisor to see that clients receive adequate service

16. With respect to supervision of Worker IV, the supervisor should   16.____

    A. show the worker that resources figures are incomplete but that even if they were complete, the family would probably be eligible for assistance

    B. ask the worker why he is so protective of these families since there are three cases so similar

    C. discuss with the worker all three cases at the same time so that the worker may see his own role in the three situations

    D. discuss with the worker the reasons for departmental policies and procedures around budgeting

17. With respect to supervision of Workers I and IV, since these two workers are friends and would seem to be influencing each other, the supervisor should   17.____

    A. hold a joint conference with them both, pointing out how they should clear with the supervisor and not make their own rules together

    B. handle the problems of each separately in individual conferences

    C. separate them by transferring one to another territory or another unit

    D. take up the problem of workers asking help of each other rather than from the supervisor in a group meeting

Questions 18-20.

DIRECTIONS: Questions 18 through 20 are to be answered SOLELY on the basis of the following passage.

One of the key supervisory problems in a large municipal recreation department is that many leaders are assigned to isolated playgrounds or small centers, where it is difficult to observe their work regularly. Often their facilities are extremely limited. In such settings, as well as in larger recreation centers, where many recreation leaders tend to have other jobs as well, there tends to be a low level of morale and incentive. Still, it is the supervisor's task to help recreation personnel to develop pride in their work and to maintain a high level of performance. With isolated leaders, the supervisor may give advice or assistance. Leaders may be assigned to different tasks or settings during the year to maximize their productivity and provide new challenges. When it is clear that leaders are not willing to make a real effort to contribute to the department, the possibility of penalties must be considered, within the scope of departmental policy and the union contract. However, the supervisor should be constructive, encourage and assist workers to take a greater interest in their work, be innovative, and try to raise morale and to improve performance in positive ways.

18. The one of the following that would be the MOST appropriate title for the above passage is   18.___

    A.   SMALL COMMUNITY CENTERS - PRO AND CON
    B.   PLANNING BETTER RECREATION PROGRAMS
    C.   THE SUPERVISOR'S TASK IN UPGRADING PERSONNEL PERFORMANCE
    D.   THE SUPERVISOR AND THE MUNICIPAL UNION - RIGHTS AND OBLIGATIONS

19. The above passage makes clear that recreation leadership performance in ALL recreation playgrounds and centers throughout a large city is   19.___

    A.   generally above average, with good morale on the part of most recreation leaders
    B.   beyond description since no one has ever observed or evaluated recreation leaders
    C.   a key test of the personnel department's effort to develop more effective hiring standards
    D.   of mixed quality, with many recreation leaders having poor morale and a low level of achievement

20. According to the above passage, the supervisor's role is to   20.___

    A.   use disciplinary action as his major tool in upgrading performance
    B.   tolerate the lack of effort of individual employees since they are assigned to isolated playgrounds or small centers
    C.   employ encouragement, advice, and, when appropriate, disciplinary action to improve performance
    D.   inform the county supervisor whenever malfeasance or idleness is detected

Questions 21-25.

DIRECTIONS: Questions 21 through 25 are to be answered SOLELY on the basis of the following passage.

EMPLOYEE LEAVE REGULATIONS

Peter Smith, as a full-time permanent city employee under the Career and Salary Plan,
earns an *annual leave allowance*. This consists of a certain number of days off a year with
pay and may be used for vacation, personal business, and for observing religious holidays.
As a newly appointed employee, during his first 8 years of city service, he will earn an annual
leave allowance of 20 days off a year (an average of 1 2/3 days off a month). After he has finished 8 full years of working for the city, he will begin earning an additional 5 days off a year.
His *annual leave allowance*, therefore, will then be 25 days a year and will remain at this
amount for seven full years. He will begin earning an additional two days off a year after he
has completed a total of 15 years of city employment. Therefore, in his sixteenth year of working for the city, Mr. Smith will be earning 27 days off a year as his *annual leave allowance* (an
average of 2 1/4 days off a month).

A sick leave allowance of one day a month is also given to Mr. Smith, but it can be used
only in cases of actual illness. When Mr. Smith returns to work after *using sick leave allowance*, he must have a doctor's note if the absence is for a total of more than 3 days, but he
may also be required to show a doctor's note for absences of 1, 2, or 3 days.

21.   According to the above passage, Mr. Smith's *annual leave allowance* consists of a cer-   21.____
tain number of days off a year which he

   A.   does not get paid for
   B.   gets paid for at time and a half
   C.   may use for personal business
   D.   may not use for observing religious holidays

22.   According to the above passage, after Mr. Smith has been working for the city for 9   22.____
years, his *annual leave allowance* will be _____ days a year.

   A.   20   B.   25   C.   27   D.   37

23.   According to the above passage, Mr. Smith will begin earning an average of 2 days off a   23.____
month as his *annual leave allowance* after he has worked for the city for full years.

   A.   7   B.   8   C.   15   D.   17

24.   According to the above passage, Mr. Smith is given a *sick leave allowance* of   24.____

   A.   1 day every 2 months   B.   1 day per month
   C.   1 2/3 days per month   D.   2 1/4 days a month

25.   According to the above passage, when he uses *sick leave allowance*, Mr. Smith may be   25.____
required to show a doctor's note

   A.   even if his absence is for only 1 day
   B.   only if his absence is for more than 2 days
   C.   only if his absence is for more than 3 days
   D.   only if his absence is for 3 days or more

KEY (CORRECT ANSWERS)

1.	C		11.	A
2.	C		12.	D
3.	D		13.	D
4.	A		14.	A
5.	B		15.	C
6.	B		16.	C
7.	A		17.	B
8.	D		18.	C
9.	B		19.	D
10.	C		20.	C

21.	C
22.	B
23.	C
24.	B
25.	A

———

TEST 3

DIRECTIONS: Questions 1 through 6 are to be answered SOLELY on the basis of the following passage.

A folder is made of a sheet of heavy paper (manila, kraft, pressboard, or red rope stock) that has been folded once so that the back is about one-half inch higher than the front. Folders are larger than the papers they contain in order to protect them. Two standard folder sizes are *letter size* for papers that are 8 1/2" x 11" and *legal cap* for papers that are 8 1/2" x 13".

Folders are cut across the top in two ways: so that the back is straight (straight-cut) or so that the back has a tab that projects above the top of the folder. Such tabs bear captions that identify the contents of each folder. Tabs vary in width and position. The tabs of a set of folders that are *one-half cut* are half the width of the folder and have only two positions.

One-third cut folders have three positions, each tab occupying a third of the width of the folder. Another standard tabbing is *one-fifth cut*, which has five positions. There are also folders with *two-fifths cut*, with the tabs in the third and fourth or fourth and fifth positions.

1. Of the following, the BEST title for the above passage is   1.____

    A. FILING FOLDERS   B. STANDARD FOLDER SIZES
    C. THE USES OF THE FOLDER   D. THE USE OF TABS

2. According to the above passage, one of the standard folder sizes is called   2.____

    A. Kraft cut   B. legal cap
    C. one-half cut   D. straight-cut

3. According to the above passage, tabs are GENERALLY placed along the _____ of the   3.____
   folder.

    A. back   B. front
    C. left side   D. right side

4. According to the above passage, a tab is GENERALLY used to   4.____

    A. distinguish between standard folder sizes
    B. identify the contents of a folder
    C. increase the size of the folder
    D. protect the papers within the folder

5. According to the above passage, a folder that is two-fifths cut has _____ tabs.   5.____

    A. no   B. two   C. three   D. five

6. According to the above passage, one reason for making folders larger than the papers   6.____
   they contain is that

    A. only a certain size folder can be made from heavy paper
    B. they will protect the papers
    C. they will aid in setting up a tab system
    D. the back of the folder must be higher than the front

Questions 7-15.

DIRECTIONS: Questions 7 through 15 are to be answered SOLELY on the basis of the following passage.

The City University of New York traces its origins to 1847, when the Free Academy, which later became City College, was founded as the first tuition-free municipal college. City and Hunter Colleges were placed under the direction of the Board of Higher Education in 1926, and Brooklyn and Queens Colleges were subsequently added to the system of municipal colleges. In 1955, Staten Island Community College, the first of the two-year colleges sponsored by the Board of Higher Education under the program of the State University of New York, joined the system.

In 1961, the four senior colleges and three community colleges then under the jurisdiction of the Board of Higher Education became the City University of New York, and a University Graduate Division was organized to offer programs leading to the Ph.D. Since then, the university has undergone even more rapid growth. Today, it consists of nine senior colleges, an upper division college which admits students at the junior level, eight community colleges, a graduate division, and an affiliated medical center.

In the summer of 1969, the Board of Higher Education resolved that the time had come to commit the resources of the university to meeting an urgent social need—unrestricted access to higher education for all youths of the City. Determined to prevent the waste of human potential represented by the thousands of high school graduates whose limited educational opportunities left them unable to meet existing admission standards, the Board moved to adopt a policy of Open Admissions. It was their judgment that the best way of determining whether a potential student can benefit from college work is to admit him to college, provide him with the learning assistance he needs, and then evaluate his performance.

Beginning with the class of June 1970, every New York City resident who received a high school diploma from a public or private high school was guaranteed a place in one of the colleges of City University.

7. Of the following, the BEST title for the above passage is   7.____

    A. A BRIEF HISTORY OF THE CITY UNIVERSITY
    B. HIGH SCHOOLS AND THE CITY UNIVERSITY
    C. THE COMPONENTS OF THE UNIVERSITY
    D. TUITION-FREE COLLEGES

8. According to the above passage, which one of the following colleges of the City University was ORIGINALLY called the Free Academy?   8.____

    A. Brooklyn College   B. City College
    C. Hunter College   D. Queens College

9. According to the above passage, the system of municipal colleges became the City University of New York in   9.____

    A. 1926   B. 1955   C. 1961   D. 1969

10. According to the above passage, Staten Island Community College came under the juris-   10.____
diction of the Board of Higher Education

    A. 6 years after a Graduate Division was organized
    B. 8 years before the adoption of the Open Admissions Policy
    C. 29 years after Brooklyn and Queens Colleges
    D. 29 years after City and Hunter Colleges

11. According to the above passage, the Staten Island Community College is   11.____

    A. a graduate division center
    B. a senior college
    C. a two-year college
    D. an upper division college

12. According to the above passage, the TOTAL number of colleges, divisions, and affiliated   12.____
branches of the City University is

    A. 18   B. 19   C. 20   D. 21

13. According to the above passage, the Open Admissions Policy is designed to determine   13.____
whether a potential student will benefit from college by PRIMARILY

    A. discouraging competition for placement in the City University among high school
       students
    B. evaluating his performance after entry into college
    C. lowering admission standards
    D. providing learning assistance before entry into college

14. According to the above passage, the FIRST class to be affected by the Open Admissions   14.____
Policy was the

    A. high school class which graduated in January 1970
    B. City University class which graduated in June 1970
    C. high school class when graduated in June 1970
    D. City University class which graduated in June 1970

15. According to the above passage, one of the reasons that the Board of Higher Education   15.____
initiated the policy of Open Admissions was to

    A. enable high school graduates with a background of limited educational opportuni-
       ties to enter college
    B. expand the growth of the City University so as to increase the number and variety
       of degrees offered
    C. provide a social resource to the qualified youth of the City
    D. revise admission standards to meet the needs of the City

Questions 16-18.

DIRECTIONS: Questions 16 through 18 are to be answered SOLELY on the basis of the fol-
                lowing passage.

Hereafter, all probationary students interested in transferring to community college
career programs (associate degrees) from liberal arts programs in senior colleges (bachelor

degrees) will be eligible for such transfers if they have completed no more than three semesters.

For students with averages of 1.5 or above, transfer will be automatic. Those with 1.0 to 1.5 averages can transfer provisionally and will be required to make substantial progress during the first semester in the career program. Once transfer has taken place, only those courses in which passing grades were received will be computed in the community college grade-point average.

No request for transfer will be accepted from probationary students wishing to enter the liberal arts programs at the community college.

16. According to this passage, the one of the following which is the BEST statement concerning the transfer of probationary students is that a probationary student   16._____

    A. may transfer to a career program at the end of one semester
    B. must complete three semester hours before he is eligible for transfer
    C. is not eligible to transfer to a career program
    D. is eligible to transfer to a liberal arts program

17. Which of the following is the BEST statement of academic evaluation for transfer purposes in the case of probationary students?   17._____

    A. No probationary student with an average under 1.5 may transfer.
    B. A probationary student with an average of 1.3 may not transfer.
    C. A probationary student with an average of 1.6 may transfer.
    D. A probationary student with an average of .8 may transfer on a provisional basis.

18. It is MOST likely that, of the following, the next degree sought by one who already holds the Associate in Science degree would be a(n)   18._____

    A. Assistantship in Science degree
    B. Associate in Applied Science degree
    C. Bachelor of Science degree
    D. Doctor of Philosophy degree

Questions 19-20.

DIRECTIONS: Questions 19 and 20 are to be answered SOLELY on the basis of the following passage.

Auto: Auto travel requires prior approval by the President and/or appropriate Dean and must be indicated in the *Request for Travel Authorization* form. Employees authorized to use personal autos on official College business will be reimbursed at the rate of 28¢ per mile for the first 500 miles driven and 18¢ per mile for mileage driven in excess of 500 miles. The Comptroller's Office may limit the amount of reimbursement to the expenditure that would have been made if a less expensive mode of transportation (railroad, airplane, bus, etc.) had been utilized. If this occurs, the traveler will have to pick up the excess expenditure as a personal expense.

Tolls, Parking Fees, and Parking Meter Fees are not reimbursable and may not be claimed.

19. Suppose that Professor T. gives the office assistant the following memorandum: 19._____
Used car for official trip to Albany, New York, and return. Distance from New York to
Albany is 148 miles. Tolls were $3.50 each way. Parking garage cost $3.00.
When preparing the Travel Expense Voucher for Professor T., the figure which should
be claimed for transportation is

   A. $120.88   B. $113.88   C. $82.88   D. $51.44

20. Suppose that Professor V. gives the office assistant the following memorandum: 20._____
Used car for official trip to Pittsburgh, Pennsylvania, and return.
Distance from New York to Pittsburgh is 350 miles. Tolls were $3.30, $11.40 going, and
$3.30, $2.00 returning.
When preparing the Travel Expense Voucher for Professor V., the figure which should
be claimed for transportation is

   A. $225.40   B. $176.00   C. $127.40   D. $98.00

Questions 21-25.

DIRECTIONS: Questions 21 through 25 are to be answered SOLELY on the basis of the following passage.

For a period of nearly fifteen years, beginning in the mid-1950's, higher education sus-
tained a phenomenal rate of growth. The factors principally responsible were continuing
improvement in the rate of college entrance by high school graduates, a 50 percent increase
in the size of the college-age (eighteen to twenty-one) group, and – until about 1967 – a rapid
expansion of university research activity supported by the Federal government.

Today, as one looks ahead to the year 2010, it is apparent that each of these favorable
stimuli will either be abated or turn into a negative factor. The rate of growth of the college-
age group has already diminished; and from 2000 to 2005, the size of the college-age group
has shrunk annually almost as fast as it grew from 1965 to 1970. From 2005 to 2010, this
annual decrease will slow down so that by 2010 the age group will be about the same size as
it was in 2009. This substantial net decrease in the size of the college-age group (from 1995
to 2010) will dramatically affect college enrollments since, currently, 83 percent of undergraduates are twenty-one and under, and another 11 percent are twenty-two to twenty-four.

21. Which one of the following factors is NOT mentioned in the above passage as contribut-   21._____
ing to the high rate of growth of higher education?

   A. A large increase in the size of the eighteen to twenty-one age group
   B. The equalization of educational opportunities among socio-economic groups
   C. The Federal budget impact on research and development spending in the higher
       education sector
   D. The increasing rate at which high school graduates enter college

22. Based on the information in the above passage, the size of the college-age group in   22._____
2010 will be

   A. larger than it was in 2009
   B. larger than it was in 1995
   C. smaller than it was in 2005
   D. about the same as it was in 2000

23. According to the above passage, the tremendous rate of growth of higher education started around   23.____

    A. 1950   B. 1955   C. 1960   D. 1965

24. The percentage of undergraduates who are over age 24 is MOST NEARLY   24.____

    A. 6%   B. 8%   C. 11%   D. 17%

25. Which one of the following conclusions can be substantiated by the information given in the above passage?   25.____

    A. The college-age group was about the same size in 2000 as it was in 1965.
    B. The annual decrease in the size of the college-age group from 2000 to 2005 is about the same as the annual increase from 1965 to 1970.
    C. The overall decrease in the size of the college-age group from 2000 to 2005 will be followed by an overall increase in its size from 2005 to 2010.
    D. The size of the college-age group is decreasing at a fairly constant rate from 1995 to 2010.

KEY (CORRECT ANSWERS)

1.	A		11.	C
2.	B		12.	C
3.	A		13.	B
4.	B		14.	C
5.	B		15.	A
6.	B		16.	A
7.	A		17.	C
8.	B		18.	C
9.	C		19.	C
10.	D		20.	B

21.	B
22.	C
23.	B
24.	A
25.	B

LIBRARY SCIENCE

TABLE OF CONTENTS

LIBRARY SCIENCE

LIBRARIES AND LIBRARIANSHIP

A. BACKGROUND

INTRODUCTION

In the history of man, the communication of ideas has been the factor which distinguishes him from the lower animals. The ability to pass on knowledge and culture through the medium of speech led to the growth of civilization. Just as important, however, was the development of a means of preserving knowledge through written records, for it is this accumulated wealth of information which has enabled man to control his environment and to uncover some of the mysteries of the earth and heavens.

Throughout recorded history, it has been the duty of the librarian to preserve and organize the books and other records which contain man's knowledge and ideas so that they may be used most effectively to further the growth of civilization.

HISTORY OF LIBRARIES

Libraries have existed ever since man has written. Ancient Egypt boasted collections of papyrus rolls, while the Babylonians and Assyrians gathered together their cuneiform covered clay tablets so that they could be cataloged and preserved. Undoubtedly, the two most famous libraries of the ancient world were at Alexandria. In the third century B.C., only a few years after their founding, the larger of the two was reported to contain over a half million papyrus rolls. Some of the earliest experiments in bibliography were the catalogs of the Alexandrian libraries.

It was in ancient Rome that public libraries flourished in abundance and that the science of librarianship became recognized. The first large book collections were acquired as the spoils of war. The Romans realized their importance and enlarged them, in addition to building library collections of their own. In the fourth century, Rome had twenty-eight public libraries. With the fall of the Empire, however, books were withdrawn to monasteries and private collections. Not until the advent of the printing press in the middle of the fifteenth century did books again become plentiful and libraries again grow.

GROWTH OF LIBRARIES IN THE UNITED STATES

There have been books and libraries in the United States since the early days of the Colonies. The first organized library was founded in 1638 at Harvard University. As other colleges were instituted in the Colonies, they too established libraries for the use of their faculties and students. Public libraries did not come as quickly. The nearest approach to public library service was the subscription library, the first being Benjamin Franklin's Library Company, organized in Philadelphia in 1731. The first public library in the United States to be directly established by state legislation was the Boston library. In 1838, Massachusetts passed legislation specifically designed to allow the city of Boston to establish a public library and to appropriate municipal funds for its support. Earlier, Peterborough, New Hampshire, formed the first tax-supported library in 1833 on the basis of a state law passed in 1821 permitting a certain portion of tax revenue to be used for schools and other educational purposes.

PROFESSIONALIZATION

The years between 1850 and 1870 saw a period of rapid growth. Not only were college and public libraries flourishing, but governmental and specialized libraries achieved importance; and as the prestige of libraries grew, so did the role of the librarian and his responsibility. Librarianship became a profession in its own right. Realizing that librarians needed an organization to help them to utilize more fully the available materials and to standardize procedures, Melvil Dewey and other prominent members of the profession called a nationwide meeting of librarians in 1876, and the American Library Association was founded. This was the first of many professional organizations which have arisen to meet the needs of librarians in the ever-widening fields of knowledge which they serve.

B. FACETS AND SCOPE OF LIBRARIANSHIP

DEMAND FOR LIBRARIANS IN THE ECONOMY

As the scope of man's knowledge has increased and as the numbers of his written works have grown, so have libraries and the need for librarians. At the first meeting of the American Library Association in 1876, only one hundred and four persons were present. At that time, there were approximately 1,000 librarians in the United States. But, by 2001, it was estimated that there were more than 150,000 active professional librarians. Public libraries, colleges, and universities, schools, governmental agencies, public and private institutions, and commercial and industrial firms all have need of the librarian's services.

In general, it may be said that librarianship is a service profession, one in which the individual, no matter what his level of responsibility or specialization, devotes his time to satisfying the needs of others to obtain informational material. Because so many of the agencies, firms, and institutions cited above have realized the importance of having trained librarians administer to the needs of their staffs, faculties, students, or patrons, the demand for librarians continues to increase. According to the United States Department of Labor, the number of librarians is expected to increase by 4.9%, while library technicians increase by 13.4% and library assistants by 12.5% by 2014.

While the largest number of 2000 graduates (32%) were placed in college and university libraries, the need for librarians in many phases of activity can be seen from the fact that 29% of the graduates accepted positions in public libraries, 21% became school librarians, and 18% undertook special and other library work.

PUBLIC LIBRARIES

The public library in the United States today is a tax-supported institution, providing direct service to all members of the community. Informational, educational, and recreational materials are available, with special programs for work with children and young people, older persons, and adult education groups. The librarians involved in these programs must be knowledgeable as to the books and other materials available and the particular psychology of the age and social groups of the people whom they are serving.

SCHOOL LIBRARIES

The school library is established by the educational governing body, usually the Board of Education, in a school community to provide books and other educational materials to the children and faculties in the elementary and secondary schools. The librarian in a school library is usually required to have a background in educational theories as well as a degree in Library Science since he or she must provide supplementary teaching aids.

COLLEGE AND UNIVERSITY LIBRARIES

The college or university library, like the school library, is established to serve the particular community of an educational institution. Research materials are stressed. In the large universities, there may be several libraries, each one serving an individual college or department, i.e., the science library, medical school library, or art school library.

SPECIAL LIBRARIES

The field of special librarianship is widely diversified. In general, there are two types of special libraries: (1) The special organization library, serving all informational needs of an organization such as a corporation or governmental agency, in which both the staff and clientele are employees of the same organization; (2) the special subject library, which may be semi-public, independent, departmental, or branch library, serving students, professional groups, or members on a given subject. The special librarian must often be a specialist in a particular field of information. He must be aware of current publications and research, and be able to assemble, organize, and maintain this information so that it may be of greatest use to the library's clientele.

THE MODERN LIBRARY

The modern library, recognizing the many media of communication available today, includes a variety of materials in its collection. Not only are books and periodicals found on library shelves, but many institutions provide audio/video material, advanced media and Internet access to patrons, along with the records, films, and slides that remain vital even in today's advanced technological age. A few public libraries have framed paintings and other pictures which may be borrowed. Braille and talking books for the blind are available, as are ceiling-projected books for the bedridden.

Modern methods are used to increase library efficiency. Microfilm and digital copies of magazines and newspapers are important space-savers, as well as effective means of preserving information. Various systems of photographic charging of materials have resulted in a saving of man-hours and an elimination of many errors.

One of the newest ways in which libraries are utilizing modern science is in the use of automatic data processing systems for library cataloging and documentation. The introduction of these new systems has been brought about by the fact that in the second half of the 20th century and into the new millennium, the production of information has accelerated with startling speed and intensity. Approximately 50% of all scholarly material available today has been produced in the last fifteen years; there are now approximately 50,000 technical journals being published, and the number is expected to increase at the rate of 1,000 yearly; in scientific areas, it has been estimated that up to 2 million articles are published yearly.

New theories are being developed and new techniques are being applied to handle this flow of information. Complex electronic and mechanical means of information storage and retrieval are being developed to organize, catalog, classify, and index the wide diversity of information.

It is in the special library, the research library, and in specialized areas of the public library where the greatest concentration of information control has taken place. A number of organizations have created large information exchange networks, spanning the continent. In the future, it is expected that countries around the world will participate in the operation of information exchange systems.

OCCUPATIONAL DESCRIPTIONS

ACQUISITIONS LIBRARIAN
0-23.10
(100.288)

OCCUPATIONAL DEFINITION

Selects and orders books, periodicals, films, and other materials for library. Reviews publishers' announcements and catalogs, and compiles lists of publications to be purchased. Compares selections with card catalog and orders-in-process to avoid duplication. Circulates selection list to branches and departments for comments. Selects vendors on basis of such factors as discount allowances and delivery dates. Compiles statistics on purchases, such as total purchases, average price, and fund allocations. May recommend acquisition of materials from individuals or organizations or by exchange with other libraries. Collaborates daily with other units, with additional library staff, and with vendors and publishers to provide optimal access to library materials for the community. Will participate in providing materials budget estimates, establishing fund allocations, monitoring expenditures, and fiscal closing.

EDUCATIONAL AND TRAINING REQUIREMENTS
Master's degree in Library Science. Training time from 1 to 2 years.

BOOKMOBILE DRIVER
7-36.260
(109.368)

OCCUPATIONAL DEFINITION

Drives bookmobile or light truck that pulls book trailer, and assists in providing library services in mobile library. Drives vehicle to specified locations on predetermined schedule. Places books and periodicals on shelves according to such groupings as subject matter, readers' age grouping, or reading level. Stamps dates on library cards, files cards, and collects fines. Compiles reports of mileage, number of books issued, and amount of fines collected. Drives vehicle to garage for repairs, such as motor or transmission overhauls, and for preventive maintenance, such as chassis lubrication and oil change. Charges and discharges library material, in a timely manner. Assists patrons in locating appropriate library materials. Responds to ready reference questions. Takes application and issues library cards.

EDUCATIONAL AND TRAINING REQUIREMENTS
Tenth grade or above. Training time approximately two months.

BOOKMOBILE LIBRARIAN
0-23.20
(100.168)

OCCUPATIONAL DEFINITION

Provides library services for mobile library within given geographical area: Surveys community needs, and selects books and other materials for library. Publicizes visits to area to stimulate reading interest. May prepare special collections for schools and other groups. May arrange bookmobile schedule. May drive bookmobile. (This job is a specialization of LIBRARIAN and shares the same basic duties.)

EDUCATIONAL AND TRAINING REQUIREMENTS
Master's degree in Library Science. Training time – three months.

CATALOGER
0-23.10
(100.388)
catalog librarian; descriptive cataloger

OCCUPATIONAL DEFINITION

Compiles information on library materials, such as books and periodicals, and prepares catalog cards to identify materials and to integrate information into library catalog: Verifies author, title, and classification number on sample catalog card received from CLASSIFIER against corresponding data on title page. Fills in additional information, such as publisher, date of publication, and edition. Examines material and notes additional information, such as bibliographies, illustrations, maps, and appendices. Copies classification number from sample card into library material for identification. Files card in assigned sections of catalog. Tabulates number of sample cards according to quantity of material and catalog subject headings to determine number of new cards to be ordered or reproduced. Prepares inventory cards to record purchase information and location of library material. Requisitions additional cards. Records new information, such as death date of author and revised edition date, to amend cataloged cards. May specialize in regularly issued publications such as journals, periodicals, and bulletins, and be known as Serials Cataloger. In some instances, depending on the needs of the particular library system, the duties of CATALOGER and CLASSIFIER are combined into one occupation given the title of CATALOGER.

EDUCATIONAL AND TRAINING REQUIREMENTS
Master's degree in Library Science. Training time – one year.

CHIEF LIBRARIAN – BRANCH OR DEPARTMENT
0-23.20
(100.168)

OCCUPATIONAL DEFINITION

Supervises staff, coordinates activities of library branch or department, and assists patrons in selection and location of books, films, audio/video items, web applications, and other materials: Trains and assigns duties to workers. Directs workers in performance of such tasks as receiving, shelving, and locating materials. Examines book reviews, publishers' catalogs, and other information sources to recommend material acquisition. Supervises and directs the arrangement of materials on shelves or in files according to classification codes, titles, or authors' names. Selects materials such as newspaper clippings and pictures to maintain special collections. Searches catalog files, biographical dictionaries, and indexes, and examines content of reference materials to assist patrons in locating and selecting materials. May assemble and arrange materials for display. May prepare replies to mail requests for information. May compile lists of library materials and recommend materials to individuals or groups and be designated Readers' -Advisory-Service Librarian. May be designated according to type of library as Chief Librarian, Branch; Chief Librarian, Bookmobile; or according to department as Chief Librarian, Art Department; Chief Librarian, Circulation Department; Chief Librarian, Music Department; Chief Librarian, Readers' Advisory Service.

EDUCATIONAL AND TRAINING REQUIREMENTS
Master's degree in Library Science. Training time of 2 to 4 years serving in various professional positions in a library system. Experience should reflect proven ability to supervise others.

CHILDREN'S LIBRARIAN
0-23.20
(100.168)

OCCUPATIONAL DEFINITION

Assists children in selecting and locating library materials, and organizes and conducts activities for children to encourage reading and use of library facilities: Confers with teachers, parents, and community groups to relate library services to the concerns of adults working with children. Stimulates children's discriminate reading by organizing such activities as story hours, reading clubs, book fairs, and summer reading programs. Shows films, tells stories, and gives book talks to encourage reading. Conducts library tours to acquaint children with library facilities and services. (This job is a specialization of LIBRARIAN and shares the same basic duties.)

EDUCATIONAL AND TRAINING REQUIREMENTS
Master's degree in Library Science. Training time, six months to one year.

CLASSIFIER
0-23.10
(100.388)
subject cataloger

OCCUPATIONAL DEFINITION

Classifies library materials such as books, films, audio/video material and periodicals according to subject matter: Reviews materials to be classified and searches information sources, such as book reviews, encyclopedias, online reference material and technical publications, to determine subject matter of materials.

Selects classification numbers and descriptive headings according to Dewey Decimal, Library of Congress, or other library classification systems. Makes sample cards containing author, title, and classification number to guide CATALOGER in preparing catalog cards for books and periodicals. Assigns classification numbers, descriptive headings, and explanatory summaries to book and catalog cards to facilitate locating and obtaining materials. Composes annotations (explanatory summaries) of material content.

EDUCATIONAL AND TRAINING REQUIREMENTS

Master's degree in Library Science. Training time from 1 to 4 years, depending on areas of responsibility, and size and complexity of library system.

COLLECTOR, OVERDUE MATERIAL
1-15.69
(240.368)

OCCUPATIONAL DEFINITION

Collects fines and overdue library material from borrowers: Sorts copies of overdue notices, according to street addresses, to plan collection route. Drives to address shown on overdue notice and explains purpose of call to borrower. Attempts to obtain overdue material and fine, or library card. Collects payment for lost material. Schedules return appointment to obtain material not on premises or advises borrower of alternative methods of returning materials. Records reasons for failure to collect material on overdue notice.

EDUCATIONAL AND TRAINING REQUIREMENTS

High school graduate. Training time, one week.

FIELD LIBRARIAN
0-23.01
(100.118)
library consultant; state field consultant

OCCUPATIONAL DEFINITION

Advises administrators, members of trustee boards, and civic groups on matters designed to improve the organization, administration, and service of public libraries: Discusses personnel staffing patterns, building plans, and book collections with administrators who request consultation service from State. Analyzes administrative policies, observes work procedures, and reviews data relative to book collections to determine effectiveness of library service to public. Compares allotments designated for building funds, salaries, and book collections with standards prepared by State agencies, to determine effectiveness of budget. Gathers statistical data, such as population and community growth rates, and analyzes building plans to determine adequacy of programs for expansion. Prepares evaluation of library systems based on observations and surveys, and recommends measures to improve organization and administration of systems according to state program for libraries and professional experience. Presents surveys of salary standards, budget analyses, and tentative building programs to administrators as suggested means of improving administration of library systems. Negotiates with civic groups, boards of trustees and library administrators who wish to consolidate library systems to resolve jurisdictional disputes and differences of opinion. Informs citizen groups of state legal requirements relative to library consolidations. Explains eligibility requirements for programs offering State and Federal financial assistance to libraries and recommends measures to be taken to attain eligibility and apply for aid. Plans and organizes programs for the recruitment of professional personnel. Directs the establishment of work procedures in new or reorganized library systems. Recommends methods of enlarging book collections. Plans and organizes training programs for administrators to inform them of recent developments in public administration and library science. Addresses town meetings and civic organizations to explain programs offered by State Division of Libraries. Occasionally demonstrates or performs all professional and clerical tasks associated with public libraries.

EDUCATIONAL AND TRAINING REQUIREMENTS
Master's degree in Library Science. Approximately five years of experience in professional library work, with at least two years as administrator.

FILM LIBRARIAN
0-23.10
(100.168)
audiovisual librarian; film-and-record librarian

OCCUPATIONAL DEFINITION
Plans film programs and keeps library of film and other audio-visual materials: Reviews records/CDs and motion-picture soundtracks, and motion pictures, considering their technical, informational, and esthetic qualities, to select materials for library collection. Prepares brief summary of film content for catalog. Prepares and arranges film programs for presentation to groups. Advises those planning to install film program on technical problems, such as acoustics, lighting, and program content, and leads discussions after film showing. May maintain or oversee maintenance of audio and video material. Operates audio/video equipment, film projectors, CD/DVD players, splicers, rewinders, and film-inspection equipment.

EDUCATIONAL AND TRAINING REQUIREMENTS
Master's degree in Library Science with additional training in film production techniques.

LIBRARIAN
0-23.20
(100.168)

OCCUPATIONAL DEFINITION

Selects and maintains library collection of books, periodicals, documents, films, recordings, media technology and other materials, and assists groups and individuals to locate and obtain materials: Furnishes information on library activities, facilities, rules, and services. Explains use of reference sources, such as bibliographic indexes, reading guides, the Internet and online applications to locate information. Describes or demonstrates procedures for searching catalog files, shelf collections and online and media applications to obtain materials. Searches catalog files and shelves to locate information. Issues and receives materials for circulation or for use in library. Assembles and arranges displays of books and other library materials. Performs variety of duties to maintain reference and circulation matter, such as copying author's name and title on catalog cards, and selecting and assembling pictures and newspaper clippings. Answers correspondence on special reference subjects. May compile book titles, bibliographies, or reading lists according to subject matter or designated interests to prepare reading lists. May select, order, catalog and classify materials. Librarians also compile lists of books, periodicals, articles, and audio-visual materials on particular subjects; analyze collections; and recommend materials. They collect and organize books, pamphlets, manuscripts, and other materials in a specific field, such as rare books, genealogy, or music. In addition, they coordinate programs such as storytelling for children and literacy skills and book talks for adults, conduct classes, publicize services, provide reference help, write grants, and oversee other administrative matters. When engaged in locating information on specific subjects is known as Reference Librarian.

EDUCATIONAL AND TRAINING REQUIREMENTS

Master's degree in Library Science. Training time of six months to two years, depending on nature of assignment.

LIBRARIAN, SPECIAL COLLECTIONS
0-23.10
(100.168)

OCCUPATIONAL DEFINITION

Collects books, pamphlets, manuscripts, and rare newspapers, to provide source material for research: Organizes collections according to field of interest. Examines reference works and consults specialists preparatory to selecting materials for collections. Compiles bibliographies. Appraises subject materials, using references, such as bibliographies, book auction records, and special catalogs. Publishes papers and bibliographies on special collections to notify clientele of available materials. Lectures on booklore, such as history of printing, bindings, and illuminations. May plan and arrange displays for library exhibits. May index and reproduce materials for sale to other libraries. May specialize in rare books and be known as Rare Book Librarian.

EDUCATIONAL AND TRAINING REQUIREMENTS
Master's degree in Library Science. Training time may range up to five years, depending on complexity of field and size of collection.

LIBRARIAN, SPECIAL LIBRARY
0-23.20
(100.118)

OCCUPATIONAL DEFINITION

Manages library or section containing specialized materials for industrial, commercial, or governmental organizations, or for such institutions as schools and hospitals: Arranges special collections of technical books, periodicals, manufacturers' catalogs and specifications, film strips, motion pictures, CD/DVD and other media, and journal reprints. Searches literature, compiles accession lists, and annotates or abstracts materials. Assists patrons in research problems. May translate or order translation of materials from foreign languages into English. May be designated according to subject matter or specialty of library or department as Art Librarian; Business Librarian; Engineering Librarian; Law Librarian; Map Librarian; Medical Librarian.

EDUCATIONAL AND TRAINING REQUIREMENTS
Master's degree in Library Science. Training time, 1 to 2 years.

LIBRARY ASSISTANT
1-20.01
(100.368)
book loan clerk; circulation clerk; desk attendant;
library aid; library attendant; library clerk; library helper

OCCUPATIONAL DEFINITION

Compiles records, sorts and shelves books, and issues and receives library materials, such as books, films, and CD-ROM: Records identifying data and due date on cards by hand or using photographic equipment to issue books to patrons. Inspects returned books for damage, verifies due date, and computes and receives overdue fines. Reviews records to compile list of overdue books and issues overdue notices to borrowers. Sorts books, publications, and other items according to classification code and returns them to shelves, files, or other designated storage area. Locates books and publications for patrons. Issues borrower's identification card according to established procedures. Files cards in catalog drawers according to system. Repairs books. Answers inquiries of nonprofessional nature on telephone and in person and refers persons requiring professional assistance to LIBRARIAN. May type material cards or issue cards and duty schedules. May be designated according to type of library as Bookmobile Clerk; Branch-Library Clerk; according to assigned department as Library Clerk, Art Department; or may be known according to tasks performed as Library Clerk, Book Return.

EDUCATIONAL AND TRAINING REQUIREMENTS
High school graduate. Training time, 6 to 12 months.

LIBRARY ASSOCIATE DIRECTOR
0-23.01
(100.118)
assistant director, library; associated librarian; deputy librarian

OCCUPATIONAL DEFINITION
Directs and assists with formulation and administration of library policies and procedures: Confers with department heads to coordinate reference services with technical processing and circulation activities. Meets with subordinate supervisory personnel to discuss goals and problems in library system. Observes functions in branch libraries to insure that established policies and work procedures are followed. Confers with LIBRARY DIRECTOR to discuss methods for increasing the efficiency of library service. Recommends reclassification of library jobs based on specific criteria of job evaluation, such as complexity of duties and scope of responsibility. Visits colleges, universities, and professional organizations to recruit workers. Forecasts growth of community from analysis of statistical data and plans building programs and expansion of library service into new areas. Acts for LIBRARY DIRECTOR in his absence.

EDUCATIONAL AND TRAINING REQUIREMENTS
Master's degree in Library Science. Training time approximately 4 to 6 years, serving in various professional and supervisory positions in a library system.

LIBRARY DIRECTOR
0-23.01
(100.118)
librarian, head; library administrator; library superintendent; manager, library

OCCUPATIONAL DEFINITION
Plans and administers program of library services: Submits recommendations on library policies and services to governing body, such as board of directors or board of trustees, and implements policy decisions. Analyzes, selects, and executes recommendations of subordinates, such as department chiefs or branch supervisors. Analyzes and coordinates departmental budget estimates and controls expenditures to administer approved budget. Reviews and evaluates orders for books, films, and advanced media, examines trade publications and samples, interviews publishers' representatives, and consults with subordinates to select materials. Administers personnel regulations, interviews and appoints job applicants, rates staff performance, and promotes and discharges employees. Plans and conducts staff meetings and participates in community and professional committee meetings to discuss library problems. Delivers book reviews and lectures to publicize library activities and services. May examine and select materials to be discarded, repaired, or replaced. May be designated according to governmental subdivision served as City-Library Director; County-Library Director.

EDUCATIONAL AND TRAINING REQUIREMENTS

Master's degree in Library Science. Training time approximately 4 to 8 years, serving in various professional and supervisory positions in a library system.

PAGE
1-23.14
(109.687)
library page; runner; shelver; shelving clerk; stack clerk

OCCUPATIONAL DEFINITION

Locates library materials such as books, periodicals, and pictures for loan, and replaces material in shelving area (stacks) or files, according to identification number and title. Trucks or carries material between shelving area and issue desk. May cut premarked articles from periodicals.

EDUCATIONAL AND TRAINING REQUIREMENTS

Tenth to twelfth grade. Training time from 1 to 3 months.

PATIENTS' LIBRARIAN
0-23.20
(100.168)
hospital librarian

OCCUPATIONAL DEFINITION

Analyzes reading needs of patients and provides library services for patients and employees in hospital or similar institution: Furnishes readers' advisory services on basis of knowledge of current reviews and bibliographies. Reviews requests, and selects books and other library materials for ward trips according to mental state, educational background, and special needs of patients. Writes book reviews for hospital bulletins or newspapers and circulates reviews among patients. Provides handicapped or bedridden patients with reading aids, such as prism glasses, page turners, book stands, or talking books, and with other audio-visual material and aids. (This job is a specialization of LIBRARIAN and shares the same basic duties. See LIBRARIAN.)

EDUCATIONAL AND TRAINING REQUIREMENTS

Master's degree in Library Science. Training time, six months.

REGISTRATION CLERK
1-20.01
(109.368)

OCCUPATIONAL DEFINITION

Registers library patrons to permit them to borrow books, periodicals, and other library materials: Copies identifying data, such as name and address, from application onto registration list and borrowers' cards to register borrowers, and issues cards to borrowers. Records changes of address or name onto registration list and borrowers' cards to amend records.

EDUCATIONAL AND TRAINING REQUIREMENTS
High school graduate. Training time, 6 to 12 months.

SCHOOL LIBRARIAN
0-23.20
(100.168)

OCCUPATIONAL DEFINITION

Provides library service which includes book and audio-visual material selection, circulation, promotional work, reference, and general administration: Serves as a resource specialist for teachers, counselors, and other faculty members. Guides students in their reading and in use of communication media. (This job is a specialization of LIBRARIAN and shares the same basic duties. See LIBRARIAN.)

EDUCATIONAL AND TRAINING REQUIREMENTS
Master's degree in Library Science. Training time of 6 months to 2 years.

SHELVING SUPERVISOR
1-20.01
(109.138)
stack supervisor

OCCUPATIONAL DEFINITION

Supervises and coordinates activities of library workers engaged in replacing books and other materials on shelves according to library classification system: Assigns duties to workers. Trains and directs workers in performance of shelving tasks. Examines materials on shelves to verify accuracy of placement. Counts number of materials placed on shelves to record shelving activity. Marks designated classification number, subject matter, or title, to arrange material for shelving.

EDUCATIONAL AND TRAINING REQUIREMENTS
High school graduate. Training time, one year.

YOUNG ADULT LIBRARIAN
0-23.10
(100.288)

OCCUPATIONAL DEFINITION

Directs young adult program in library to provide special activities for high school and college-age readers: Organizes young adults activities, such as chess clubs, creative writing club, and photography contests. Contacts speakers, writes and distributes advertising, and meets young adult club representatives to prepare group programs. Delivers talks on books to stimulate reading. Addresses groups such as parent-teacher associations and civic organizations, to inform community of activities. Conducts high school classes on Library Tours to acquaint students with library facilities and services. Compiles lists of young adult reading materials for individuals, high school classes, and branch libraries. Issues and receives library materials, such as books and phonograph records. (This job is a specialization of LIBRARIAN and shares the same basic duties. See LIBRARIAN.)

EDUCATIONAL AND TRAINING REQUIREMENTS
Master's degree in Library Science with an additional one year training time.